THE LANGUAGE OF GOD

A Companion Dictionary to the Bible

Dr. JAMES B SCOTT

VIDE

Vide Press
6200 Second Street
Washington D.C. 20011
www.VidePress.com

ISBN: 978-1-954618-41-1

Printed in the United States of America

Cover by Miblart.com

In Loving Memory of
the Reverend Doctor
Molly Davis Scott

[illegible] James B Scott

Contents

The Purpose of this Book

Language: 1 a) human speech b) the ability to communicate by this means c) a system of vocal sounds and combinations of such sounds to which meaning is attributed, used for the expression or communication of thoughts and feelings d) the written representation of such a system (*Webster's Dictionary*).

God: 1 any of various beings conceived of as supernatural, immortal, and having special powers over the lives and affairs of people and the course of nature; typically considered objects of worship **2** an image that is worshiped: idol **3** person or thing or thing deified or excessively honored and admired **4** in monotheistic religions, the creator and ruler of the universe, regarded as eternal, infinite, and all-powerful, and all-knowing; Supreme Being; the Almighty (*Webster's Dictionary*).

"God, who at various times and in various ways spoke in time past to the fathers by the prophets, has in these last days spoken to us by His Son, whom He has appointed heir of all things, through whom also He made the worlds:" (Hebrews 1:1-2).

Recording and quoting all the *"various times and in various ways"* would require innumerable books. The sixty-six books which compose the Bible were affirmed as being authentic by the Early Church and are the histories and testimonies of God's spoken word and loving actions.

The Bible contains God's communication with us humans. It is therefore imperative we reclaim, relearn, understand, and use the language of our Christian heritage to understand that which is being communicated. Having a common historical interpretation of the keywords (language) is necessary for understanding the context and meaning in which they are used and their application in our lives. While many words may be familiar, other words may not. The brief definitions are meant to increase the ability to understand, experience, and communicate not only the primary concepts of the Christian faith but the truth of the Living God.

Dictionary

[A] **1. Adoption:** *"But when the fullness of time had come, God sent His Son, born of a woman, born under the law . . . so that we might receive adoption as children."* (Galatians 4:4-5). *"For you did not receive the spirit of bondage again to fear, but you received the Spirit of adoption by whom we cry out, 'Abba, Father.'"* (Romans 8:15).

In the Christian world adoption is a beautiful and wonderful word. Adoption is a key concept in the New Covenant, recently now (Twentieth Century) commonly called the New Testament (testimony/ witness). It is meant to express God's desire to give us the status as sons and daughters and co-heirs with Christ. In the world in which the Early Church existed, adoption gave the adopted person the same legal status and rights as naturally born children. Our salvation, our receiving and becoming like Christ, endows us with adoption and all the benefits, present and eternal (Galatians 3:26; 4:4-7; Romans 8:17, 38-39; John 1:12).

Remember: God's love wants to adopt us as His own legal children so that we might become heirs with Christ and enjoy eternal life.

2. Angels: *"Then the devil left Him (Jesus), and behold angels came and ministered to Him."* (Matthew 4:11).

"Likewise, I say to you, there is joy in the presence of the angels of God, over one sinner who repents." (Luke 15:10). *"Take heed that you do not despise one of these little ones, for I say to you that in heaven their angels always see the face of My Father who is in heaven."* (Matthew 18:10).

Angels were created by God as "messengers" and "guardians" to and for humans. Angels can be seen working in both the Old Testament and the New. In the Old Testament we see how some angels fell into rebellion and thereby caused sin and death to enter the world—our world. Angels are supernaturally gifted with wisdom and intelligence and are sent by God to aid us both personally and in the Church (Hebrews 1:14). Angels are sent as guardians, especially for children (Matthew 18:10). Angels are meant to be present with believers at death (Luke 16:22). The New Testament has well over 150 references to angels, a clear indicator of their reality and importance.

Remember: Angels are real and present in the world and in our lives.

3. Anointed: *"Is anyone among you sick? Let him call for the elders of the church, and let them pray over him, anointing him with oil in the name of the Lord. And the prayer of faith will save the sick, and the Lord will raise him up. And if he has committed sins, he will be forgiven."* (James 5:14-15). *"Now He who establishes us with you in Christ and has anointed us is God, who also has sealed us and given us the Spirit in our hearts as a guarantee."* (2 Corinthians 1:21-22).

The first use of the term applies to the ordinary physical aspect of the washing of the body or the application to the sick. The substance applied is, with rare exceptions, oil. In the Old Testament: Ruth 3:3; 2 Samuel 12:20; Daniel 10:3; and Micah 6:15. In the New Testament: Matthew 6:17; Luke 7:38, 46; John 11:2; 12:3; Mark 6:13; 16:1; and James 5:14. A second use refers to sacred or symbolic anointing. Again, the substance used is oil. The word is used in the anointing of kings, priests, prophets, and believers. The anointing was the blessing of God and the selection for a sacred purpose. In the Old Testament: 1 Samuel 10:1; Exodus 28:41; and 1 Kings 19:16. Christ is called the "Anointed One" in the New Testament: Acts 4:26–27; 2 Corinthians 1:21. In James 5:14, the anointing with oil for the sick was the visible means of the action of the Holy Spirit. In all three streams of Christendom, the anointing with oil is practiced for healing and for the prevention and cure of the sick. Anointed is still many times used to describe a person who had or who has an extraordinary gift and contribution to the Kingdom of God.

Remember: The Holy Spirit power of God's anointing is still present today.

4. Antinomianism: *"You shall not do as we are doing here today—everyone doing what is right in their own eyes."* (Deuteronomy 12:8). Jesus said, *"Beware of false prophets, who come to you in sheep's clothing, but inwardly are ravenous wolves."* (Mathew 7:15). *"But there were also false prophets among the people, even as there will be false teachers among you, who will secretly bring in deceptive heresies."* (2 Peter 2:1).

This word does not appear in the Bible. The concept is meant to include several behaviors that the Church has always declared are aberrant or destructive to the teaching and life of the Christian faith. The word actually means "against the law". One group the Early Church fought against was a group of people called Gnostics. (Jude 4-19 and 2 Peter 2). Gnostics believed they had special knowledge, insight and interpretation of the Bible. The Gnostics believed that because of God's great grace we are therefore freed from the rules and requirements of biblical commands. In every century the Church has contended with people who believe they have received a special "new revelation" and interpretation of Scripture with the outcome being the freedom from what they perceive as antiquated rules and expectations of teaching, life, and behavior (Doctrine and Discipline).

Remember: Beware of those who have a new special revelation from God. The Old and New Testaments, meaning the Bible, and the Holy Spirit's teaching in the Tradition of the Church are all that is necessary for the faith and practice of holiness.

5. Apostles: *"And when He* (Jesus) *had called His twelve disciples to Him, He gave them power over unclean spirits, to cast them out, and to heal all kinds of sickness and all kinds of disease. Now the names of the twelve apostles are these . . ."* (Matthew 10:1-2). *"These twelve Jesus sent out and commanded them, saying:"* (Matthew 10:5).

The word means "to send" or "to be sent". The word is almost exclusively found in New Testament writings.

Jesus is understood to be the first apostle sent by the Father. (Hebrews 3:1). It is understood that Jesus as the first representative sent by God has the authority and power of that position as the first apostle. Jesus then calls and designates the Twelve as His apostles, giving them authority and power to represent Him. (Mark 3:14-15; 6:30). The word Apostle is meant to be exclusive of the Twelve with the exception of Paul. Paul had a specific calling from Jesus (Galatians 1:1) which was honored by the apostles at the Jerusalem Church. Paul was the "apostle" to the Gentiles, but he was not seen as one of the Twelve. The word disciple is seen as a different designation although on occasion the Twelve are called disciples.

Remember: To honor and learn from the First Apostles, the Twelve, and Paul, all whom were called and sent by God

6. Ascension: *"Jesus said to her, 'Mary'!" She turned and said to Him, "Rabbani" (which is to say, Teacher). 'Do not cling to Me, for I have not yet ascended to My Father; but go to my brethren and say to them, I am ascending to My Father and your Father, and to My God and your God.'"*(John 20:16-17). *"No one has ascended to heaven but He who came down from heaven, that is, the Son of Man who is in heaven."* (John 3:13).

The Ascension refers to the physical departure of Jesus from His earthly experience. (Luke 24:51; Acts 1:9). Jesus ascended into heaven on the fortieth day after His resurrection (Acts 1:3) and before the descent of the Holy Spirit at Pentecost (Acts 2:1). Jesus' ascension heralded the sending of the Holy Spirit. Ascension Day is the fortieth day after Easter. Christ is now our representative in heaven. (Romans 8:34; I John 2:1; Hebrews 7:25).

Remember: Just as Jesus ascended to heaven we will have our own personal Ascension Day.

7. Assurance: *"Therefore, brethren, having boldness to enter the Holiest by the blood of Jesus, by a new and living way, which He consecrated for us, through the veil, that is, His flesh, and having a High Priest over the house of God, let us draw near with a true heart in full assurance of faith . . ."* (Hebrews 10:19-22). *"But as many as received Him, to them He gave the right to become children of God, to those who believe in His name: who were born, not of blood, nor of the will of the flesh, nor of the will of man, but of God."* (John 1:12-13).

The first use applies to the meaning of guarantee or certitude (Acts 17:3). Christ being raised from the dead guarantees the truth that Christ will come again to judge the world. A second use understands that we can have complete confidence in expecting that God will completely fulfill His promises (Hebrews 6:11; 10:22; and 1 Thessalonians 1:5). A third understanding that has special importance is the confidence of the pardon of our sins and our place in the Kingdom of God. It is the conviction given to us by the Holy Spirit that indeed we are children of God. (Romans 8:26–27).

Remember: We can have assurance of our salvation and future reward; as long as we have made Jesus Lord and are following Jesus commands we do not have to live in fear of whether or not we are saved, that we are children of God, and that we will inherit eternal life.

8. Atonement See *Sacrifice of Christ.*

[B] **9. Baptism**: *"Then Jesus came from Galilee to John at the Jordan to be baptized by him. And John tried to prevent Him saying, 'I need to be baptized by You, and are You coming to me?' But Jesus answered and said to him, 'Permit it to be so now, for thus it is fitting for us to fulfill all righteousness.'"* (Matthew 3:14-15). *"Or do you not know that as many of us as were baptized into Christ Jesus were baptized into His death? Therefore we were buried with Him through baptism into death, that just as Christ was raised from the dead by the glory of the Father, even so we also should walk in newness of life."* (Romans 6:3-4).

To baptize means literally to immerse, to put into or under. In the New Covenant, baptism is the means of grace by which we enter the Kingdom of God (John 3:5), are joined in Christ (Romans 6:3), and are granted remission of our sins and the gift of the Holy Spirit (Acts 2:38). In Methodism as in the major Christian denominations all three modes are offered, baptism by immersion, by aspersion, commonly called sprinkling; and by effusion, commonly called pouring; and we baptize "in the name of the Father, and of the Son, and of the Holy Spirit" (Matthew 28:19). In the Old Testament, baptism was pictured by the passage of God's people with Moses through the Sea of Reeds—the Red Sea (1 Corinthians 10:1–2). John the Baptist, the last prophet of the Old Covenant, baptized in water unto repentance (Mark 1:4; Acts 19:4).

John's baptism was received by Jesus, who thereby transformed the water and the baptism itself into the symbol of His life, death, and resurrection. The essence of baptism is our death, burial, and resurrection in union with Jesus Christ. It is a rite of passage, given by Christ to the Church, as an entrance into the Kingdom of God and eternal life. The apostle Paul described the promise of God in this mystery most succinctly when he wrote, *"Therefore we were buried with Him through baptism unto death, that just as Christ was raised from the dead by the glory of the Father, even so we also should walk in newness of life"* (Romans 6:4). The manner of baptism requires only the use of water in some way and invoking the name of Jesus, according to classic Christian theology, though Jesus said for us to baptize in the name of the Trinity. Wesleyan Methodists as do Roman Catholics and Orthodox Catholics, Anglicans, Lutherans, Presbyterians, and others believe in baptizing babies because baptism is a covenant between God, the Christian parents, and the community of faith. Some denominations will not baptize until a person is old enough to speak for himself. Question 258 of *The Larger Catechism* of the Methodist Episcopal Church asks, *"Do the Holy Scriptures give us authority for infant baptism?" The answer given is, "Undoubtedly (yes) . . . when we read of the apostles baptizing whole families (Acts xvi, 15-33; I Cor. 1, 16) we may justly infer that little children were also baptized."* Most Christians agree that baptism is a one-time happening and that to re-baptize would negate the original baptism.

Remember: Our baptism in Christ is meant to cleanse and begin to form us in Christ's image. In other words we are to become like Christ in His holiness and members of the One, Holy, Catholic, Apostolic Church of Jesus Christ.

10. Baptism of the Holy Spirit: *"And being assembled together with them, He (*Jesus*) commanded them not to depart from Jerusalem, but to wait for the Promise of the Father, 'which' He said, 'you have heard from Me'; for John truly baptized with water, but you shall be baptized with the Holy Spirit not many days from now."* (Acts 1:4-5).

The Holy Spirit was present at Creation. (Genesis 1:2). The Holy Spirit is co-equal with the Father and the Son and of the same substance. The Holy Spirit has been extremely active in history, especially during times of renewal. That was true of the Wesleyan/ Methodist holiness/evangelical movement of the Eighteenth and Nineteenth Centuries. In essence, it was a truly Orthodox (right doctrine and discipline) movement in the traditional character of the One, Holy, Catholic, and Apostolic Church of the first centuries. In the Old Testament, the Holy Spirit promised that the coming of the Son would also by Jesus' proclamation be an outpouring of that same Spirit. (Isaiah 11:2; 61:1-3).The prophets prophesied the same promise. (Joel 2:28-29; Ezekiel 36:26-27). In the New Testament we see a supernatural and dramatic descent of the Holy Spirit at Jesus' baptism (Matthew 3:16; Mark 1:10, Luke 3:22). A new day had dawned on the world. John lifted up a new understanding of Spirit baptism. As did Jesus (Acts 1:5), as did Peter (Acts 11:16), John (Acts 1:26, 33), and Paul (Acts 19:4-6; 1 Corinthians 12:13). Water baptism was the initiation of a person into the covenantal community of Christ. Pentecost ushered in a Spirit baptism that initiated a new indwelling of the Spirit called a baptism "in", or "with", or "filling" of the Holy Spirit. The end result of this baptism was that we could become a holy people, exhibiting the fruits of the Spirit and the gifts of the Spirit. In mind, heart, and soul, we are meant to become like Jesus. And it is the Spirit who will lead and cause this transformation to happen. In some Pentecostal groups there has been an emphasis on the supernatural gifts of healing, tongues, prophesy, etc. In every historical renewal of the Church there has been an extraordinary manifestation of the supernatural. This was true of the Evangelical Awakening of the Eighteenth and Nineteenth Centuries with both the First and Second Great Awakenings. There is no biblical reason to think that the Spirit is confined by what He has or has not done before. In these dark times, I would hope we Christians will all pray for another supernatural outpouring of the Spirit on us and on the Church of Jesus Christ.

Remember: We are meant to have a living personal relationship with the Spirit, Him living in us and us in Him. It is the Spirit who called us to repentance, it is the Spirit who is leading us in our growth in holiness. As Jesus is our friend, so too the Spirit is our friend.

11. Biblical Worldview: *"Then Jesus spoke to them again, 'I am the light of the world. He who follows Me shall not walk in darkness but have the light of life.'"* (John 8:12). Jesus said, *"No one can serve two masters; for either he will hate the one and love the other, or else he will be loyal* *to the one and despise the other. You cannot serve God and mammon."* (Matthew 6:24).

The world can be a very deceptive place. God loves His world and sent Jesus not to condemn it but to save it (John 3:16). The word "worldview" is not found in the Bible. It is only meant as a way or a lens at looking at the Kingdom of God and the world. We all have a certain "lens" with which we see and evaluate. Having a biblical worldview, means looking at the world through "the light of life" and infers that we make God's scriptures, Jesus' example, and the Holy Spirit's leading the template by which we live, make decisions, and guide our lives in accordance with God's higher values and purposes. The purpose of a biblical worldview is to see and understand reality in the world, see and understand ourselves, and make our life and faith decisions in light of Scripture. Loyalty to Jesus demands full allegiance. We cannot give full allegiance to the powers and things of the world and to the Kingdom of God. We are meant to enjoy the things of the world and we are meant to be active in the world just not give our allegiance to it. In the world but not of the world. Our allegiance and our life, our personhood, our citizenship, and our future are in another world.

Remember: We are to understand ethics, morality, values, our life through the vision of the Kingdom of God not the Kingdom of the world.

12. Bishops: *"Paul and Timothy, bondservants of Jesus Christ, To all the saints in Philippi, with the bishops and* *deacons."* (Philippians 1:1). *"This is a faithful saying: If a man desires the position of a bishop, he desires a good work."* (1 Timothy 3:1).

The word bishop is a word that came from the culture as opposed to the word elder which was a biblical word from the Old Testament. The word bishop literally means "overseer". It became a designation for "pastor" or "shepherd". In Acts 20:17-28 and Titus 1:5-7. the word described the function of an elder sometimes called presbyter. By the end of the First Century each church had one or more bishops. Presbyters (elders) and deacons were ordained orders. Bishops were and are elders who are elected and appointed to serve the function of an overseer for the clergy and congregation or later several congregations. Bishops are the "First" among "Equals". Thus there developed the three functions of clergy: bishops, elders, and deacons. 1 Timothy 3:2 and Titus 1:7 outline qualifications for a bishop. Bishops were elected because of their holiness, services as theologians, abilities to teach and pastor, and maintaining discipline. Bishops were universal in the church until the Sixteenth Century Reformation when some protestant denominations eliminated that office.

Remember: Bishops, as well as elders and deacons are expected to lead exemplary lives of holiness of heart and life; are expected to be theologically astute and maintain the doctrine and discipline of the One, Holy, Catholic, and Apostolic Church as expressed in the Bible and the Creeds of the Church.

13. Breaking of the Bread: *"And they continued steadfastly in the apostles' doctrine and fellowship, in the breaking of bread, and in prayers."* (Acts 2:42). *"Give us this day our daily bread."* (Matthew 6:11).

These words expressed in Acts 2:42 refer to what is commonly called the Lord's Supper, the Holy Communion, the Eucharist, the Mass, Etc. *See Eucharist.*

[C] **14. Calling**: *"And Jesus walking by the Sea of Galilee, saw two brothers, Simon called Peter, and Andrew his brother, casting a net into the sea; for they were fishermen. Then He said to them, 'Follow me and I will make you fishers of men.' They immediately left their nets and followed Him. Going on from their He saw two other brothers, James the son of Zebedee, and John his brother, in the boat with Zebedee their father, mending their nets. He called them, and immediately they the boat and their father, and followed Him."* (Matthew 4:18-22).

There are several words in the Scripture that refer to the words *call, called,* or *calling*. In the beginning God called the light and it became day. God called/chose/elected the Israelites to a specific heritage and task. There is a specific word that refers to God's call or invitation to respond to the grace of salvation (Romans 8:30; 11:29; 1 Corinthians 1:9, 26; 1 Thessalonians 2:12; Hebrews 9:15). Without going into detail, the manner in which the word is used implies a call/calling to a purpose, destiny, or vocation. Examples of the manner in which it is used would be Ephesians 1:18, Jesus calling; Philippians 23:14, high calling; 2 Thessalonians 1:11, your calling;

2 Timothy 1:9, holy calling; Hebrews 3:1, heavenly calling; and Ephesians 4:1, the calling with which you were called. We are called to respond to the Gospel of Jesus Christ (Matthew 20:16; 22:14; 1 Corinthians 1:2, 24). In another way we are called to apostleship (Romans 1:1; 1 Corinthians 1:1). In essence, God is calling/choosing/electing us to respond to the gift of salvation. The calling then to be a Christian is one sense of the calling. The calling to a specific task is another dimension of our calling. The calling to be a follower of Jesus never changes. Our specific calling to a vocation or task will change. The act of the calling is God or Christ or the Holy Spirit revealing Himself to us as an invitation or a demand to become something or do something or a vision or an idea that we are to accomplish. Its form is most often a sense of God's presence and an assurance, a firm knowledge that we "know what we know." It may arrive through a thought in our head, a dream in our sleep, another person, a feeling in our prayer time, a clarity when reading scripture, or a message through worship, sermon, music, or just in an unusual flash of insight.

Remember: God has called,chosen,elected, and gifted each one of us to become like Jesus and do good works. Knowing who we are and how we are gifted will help lead us in the path of holiness, happiness, and productivity.

15. Casual Christian: *"For men will be lovers of themselves, lovers of money . . . lovers of pleasure . . . having the form of godliness but denying its power. And from such people turn away."* (2 Timothy 3:1-5).

This term "Casual Christian" is a reference to one of Reverend John Wesley's most well-known sermons, *The Almost Christian*. The Reverend John Wesley was the Anglican Priest who started the Methodist Societies within the Anglican Church which eventually became the Methodist Church. Rev. Wesley died an Anglican priest. The sermon and term is based on Acts 26:28. "Then (King) Agrippa said unto Paul, '*Almost thou persuadest me to be a Christian.*'" [KJV]. Wesley then enjoined his hearers to move from "almost Christian" to "altogether Christian." For Wesley, an almost Christian—what we are calling a Casual Christian—can be a "heathen" (an unbeliever) who does no harm and in fact does some good, or can be a somewhat believer who has the outside of being a "real Christian" without having the inside of the same. The Casual Christian might never take the Lord's name in vain, might avoid small and large sins of all types, may help some people, use all the means of grace, and be sincere in "doing good . . . abstaining from evil . . . using the ordinances of God." However this well-intentioned person never partakes of the fullest of God. Mr. Wesley declared that he spent most of the first thirty years of his life as an almost Christian. *See Complete Christian.*

Remember: There is no such thing as a half Christian. It is decisive to know how to be a Complete Christian in order to experience all the benefits and rewards of the Christian life.

16. Christ: *"When Jesus came into the region of Caesarea Philippi, He asked His disciples . . . He said to them,*

'But who do you say I am?' Simon Peter answered and said, 'You are the Christ, the Son of the Living God.' Jesus answered and said to him, 'Blessed are you Simon Bar-Jonah, for flesh and blood has not revealed this to you, but My Father who is in heaven.'" (Matthew 16:13-17).

This is the English form of the Greek verb *Christos,* which means "anointed." An equivalent word is the Jewish word *Messiah.* In the O.T., the prophets were called the "Anointed of God" (Psalm 105:15). In the New Testament, Jesus accepted the use of the term as a title three times (Matthew 16:17; Mark 14:61–62; John 4:26). Jesus spoke of Himself as the Christ (Acts 9:34). For other uses see Matthew 1:17; 11:2; John 17:3; Romans 6:4; 7:4; 8:9; 9:5; 15:19; 17; 1 Corinthians 1:2, 3:11; Galatians 2:16; and 1 John 5:6.

Remember: Jesus' name is not Jesus Christ. Jesus is *the* Christ, *the* Messiah, *the* Anointed One prescribed in the Old Covenant and now personally revealed and realized in the New Covenant.

17. Chrismation: *"Now when the apostles who were at Jerusalem heard that Samaria had received the word of God, they sent Peter and John to them, who, when they had come down, prayed for them that they might receive the Holy Spirit. For as yet He had fallen upon none of them. They had only been baptized in the name of the Lord Jesus. Then they laid hands on them, and they received the Holy Spirit."* (Acts: 8:14-17). *"You have an anointing* (chrisma) *from the Holy One and know all things."* (1 John 2:20).

The Early Church carried on this Baptism by the Holy Spirit by what was called Chrismation. In the Early Church, immediately after water baptism, a child or adult was "chrismated" which meant confirmed. The priest would take a special ointment of oil called the Chrism and anoint the newly baptized with the sign of the cross saying "The seal of the gift of the Holy Spirit." The person who had been incorporated into Christ at baptism had now received the gift of the Holy Spirit. *"You have an anointing* (chrisma) *from the Holy One and know all things."* (1 John 2:20). In both the Roman Catholic Church of the West and the Orthodox Catholic Church of the East, chrismation is by a bishop. In the Orthodox Church, the person, whether adult or child, receives Holy Communion immediately after chrismation.

Remember: It is decisive to be baptized into Christ and also to be baptized with *"the seal of the gift of the Holy Spirit."*

18. Church (Body of Christ): *"Now, therefore, you are no longer strangers and foreigners, but fellow citizens with the saints and members of the household of God, having been built on the foundation of the apostles and prophets, Jesus Christ Himself being the chief cornerstone, in whom the whole building, being fitted together, grows into a holy temple in the Lord, in whom you also are being built together for a dwelling place of God in the Spirit."* (Ephesians 2:19-22). *"For as we have many members in one body, but all the members do not have the same function, so we, being many, are one body in Christ, and individually members one of another."* (Romans 12:4-5).

The Greek word out of which the word *Church* came is *ekklesia*. The word itself literally is *ek* (out of) and *klesis* (a calling). The people of God are thus both "called out" of the world and then "called out" of the Church into the world. The word was used by the Greeks for an assembly of people who were "called out" and met for a designated purpose. In the Old Testament, the two Hebrew words that became translated as *ekklesia* were words used to designate the gathering of Israel. In Acts 7:38, the word is used for Israel. There are two applications for us. One is that the word refers to the whole company of Christ. In Matthew 16:18, Jesus said, *"I will build My Church."* It further is used to describe the Body of Christ (Ephesians 1:22; 5:23). The believers of Jesus saw themselves first of all as a whole that belonged to Christ and made up His Body. The second application is to the singular gathering as we see in Matthew 18:17. It always refers to a gathering of professed believers (Acts 20:28; 1 Corinthians 1:2; Galatians 1:13; 1 Thessalonians 1:1; 2 Thessalonians 1:1; 1 Timothy 3:5). The emphasis here is that the local assembly always saw itself as a representative and subservient part of the whole Body of Christ. Each part made up the whole, and the New Testament Christians could never perceive themselves as being an independent body of believers. In the simplest form it is the company of believers in Christ who have experienced the symbolic rite of death and resurrection through baptism, have received new life through Jesus Christ, have become a new creation through the gift of the Holy Spirit, have gathered for worship and celebration through the Holy Eucharist, and are being prepared to be sent into the world for the work of evangelism and serving Christ in the world.

Remember: Jesus was emphatic in teaching that there is no such thing as an individual follower of Him. To be in Christ is to be in the *ecclesia*, the One, Holy, Catholic, and Apostolic Church of Jesus the Christ in whichever one of the three branches of Christianity: Roman, Orthodox, or Protestant.

19. Connexion: *"For as the body is one and has many members, but all the members of that one body, being many, are one body, so also is Christ. For by one Spirit we were all baptized into one body—whether Jews or Greeks, whether slaves or free—and have all been made to drink into one Spirit. For in fact the body is not one member but many."* (1 Corinthians 12:12-14).

The word *connexion* is an old word that comes out of antiquity reflecting a connection that implies immersion with two or more people or objects. Spelling *connection* with an "x" instead of a "t" was the old European spelling of the word. The word has a special meaning of being uniquely connected to someone or something. In the origin of the word we find it was used for religious groups that had a special love and devotion to each other. Christians of all backgrounds and theological interpretations should have a special feeling of love and community because all are connected together in the Vine, Jesus Christ, who is the Head of the Body. That is the Connexion: connected to the Trinity, to other Christians/the Church, to the world in service.

The word *Connexion* took on a specific religious connotation during the eighteenth and nineteenth centuries. Small Bible study groups, prayer groups, or other groups within a denomination formed circuits that would employ traveling ministers to preach or to bring special knowledge or skills to their circuit. These ministers usually worked in conjunction with the minister assigned to the parish. These circuits became known as a Connexion. Hence, in the 1700s, the Wesleyan societies, classes, and conferences became known as the Methodist Connexion. After the death of the Reverend John Wesley, a series of Methodist groups emerged from the Anglican Church. The groups retained the name *Connexion.* Examples are: the Methodist New Connexion, the Primitive Methodist Connexion, and the Countess of Huntingdon's Connexion. The Methodist Church of Great Britain still uses the term Connexion explaining that the circuits, districts, and conferences form the Connexion. The concept of a connectional system is very different from a congregational system. Every single person, every local congregation, every district, every conference is joined as one with Christ in Christ's mission in the world. No one is ever independent. The term was used extensively with Christian groups and denominations in the United States until the 1900s when the word was lost. Perhaps the concept was lost also. However, the word is still used today in a multitude of other contexts. We are devoutly Methodist but not Methodist only since the Methodist Connexion is truly joined together as one in Christ's global Christian Connexion.

Remember: To be in love with Jesus is to be in love with His Connexion, His people of whatever denomination or group in whatever part of the world.

20. Conversion: *"Restore me to the joy of your salvation, And uphold me by Your generous Spirit, Then I will teach transgressors Your ways, And sinners will be converted to You."* (Psalm 51:12-13). Jesus said, *"Assuredly, I say to you, unless you are converted and become as little children, you will by no means enter the kingdom of heaven."* (Matthew 18:3). *"Repent therefore and be converted, that your sins may be blotted out, so that times of refreshing may come from the presence of the Lord."* (Acts 3:19).

The word is found in two different ways in the New Testament. The word *turn* is translated as "be converted" (Matthew 18:3). To turn about, to turn toward, to turn around. (5:19, 20). The word implies a deliberate act or movement of turning from one way to another or of leaving one place and going to another (Matthew 13:15; Mark 4:12; Luke 22:32; Acts 3:19; 28:27). It later became a word to denote the change of a person from one state to another state. Conversion in the Christian sense is such a radical turn that it is described as a "new birth" or "new creation." The question then is, "What causes someone to want to be converted?" What causes a person to make a radical life "turn" from one way of life to another? It is not just an intellectual casual decision but rather a radical change of heart, mind, and soul that can take place at almost any age and under any condition. But it is a radical change of the person. For some people it is a dramatic time-remembered event.

For some people it is a slow evolving event or series of events that culminate in an "aha" moment.

Remember: However we describe our "conversion" it is an ongoing unfolding from one state to another. Becoming like Christ is an ongoing change in our holiness.

21. Complete Christian: *"Jesus answered him, 'The first of all the commandments is; Hear, O Israel, the Lord our God is one. And you shall love the Lord your God with all your heart, with all your soul, with all your mind, and with all your strength. This the first commandment. And the second, like it, is this; You shall love your neighbor as yourself. There is no other commandment greater than these.'"* (Mark 12:29-31). *"But we all, with unveiled face, beholding as though in a mirror the glory of the Lord, are being transformed into the same image from glory to glory, just as by the Spirit of the Lord."* (2 Corinthians 3:18).

The Complete Christian is Mr. Wesley's "altogether Christian." This is the believer who loves God with all one's heart, soul, mind, and strength and more than anyone or anything else. This is the person who loves their neighbor as much as they love self, sees the whole world as their neighbor, and loves as Christ loves. 1 Corinthians 13 describes that type of love: long-suffering, gentle, not jealous or envious, seeking good for others, rejoicing in truth, as well as believing, hoping, and enduring all things. Mr. Wesley says that the complete, altogether Christian truly believes the Holy Scriptures, the testimony of the Holy Spirit in history through the martyrs, the Ecumenical Councils, and the Creeds are true. The complete, altogether Christian is confident that through faith in Christ, one's sins are forgiven, is saved from eternal damnation into eternal life, is reconciled to find the favor of God, and wants to obey God's commandments. Complete Christians are found in every denomination and every community of believers.

Remember: We can have the assurance of being a Complete Christian by loving God and neighbor with all our heart, soul, mind, and strength, growing in His image, and obeying Jesus' commands.

22. Core Beliefs/Doctrine: *"Now, about the middle of the feast Jesus went up into the temple and taught. And the Jews marveled, saying, 'How does this Man know letters, having never studied?' Jesus answered them and said, 'My doctrine is not mine but His who sent Me.'"* (John 7:14-16). *"If you instruct the brethren in these things, you will be a good minister of Jesus Christ, nourished in the words of faith and of the good doctrine which you have carefully followed . . . Take heed to yourself and to the doctrine. Continue in them for in doing this you will save both yourself and those who hear you."* (1 Timothy 4:6, 16). *"Whoever transgresses and does not aid in the doctrine of Christ does not have God. He who abides in the doctrine of Christ has both the father and the Son."* (2 John: 9).

The key question is, "What is the true doctrine of Christ?" and therefore, "What do I believe to be true?" "What do I believe, teach, and live by?" These questions determine our behavior. Identifying my core beliefs, writing them down, and exploring whether I really believe they are true and accurate will show what drives my decisions and my behavior. For example, my emotions and behavior will be one way to see if I believe that God is in control of history and the world versus if I believe God created the world but is not involved in human existence. The way I deal with a difficult person in my life would vary one way or another depending on whether or not I believe that it is possible for people to change. It may depend on whether I have been forgiven and am able therefore to forgive and love others. What we are looking for is not every opinion we have, but the essential core beliefs we hold about God, people, life, and ourselves that are most important and that inform other beliefs we hold. The true doctrine of Christ is not negotiable and is critical to our salvation.

Remember: It is absolutely necessary for our salvation to know what the essential core beliefs (Doctrine of Christ) are and what beliefs are negotiable. That is the only way we can discern what is true and what is false and not be confused or misled and fall.

23. Core Values: *"You will know them by their fruits. Even so, every good tree bears good fruit; but a bad tree bears bad fruit. Therefore by their fruits you shall know them."* (Matthew 7:16, 17, 18, 20).

Examining my *behavior*s that derive from my beliefs will identify my core values, my deepest values and will determine my fruit. We might say we value our children, but the calendar of the past month shows so little time spent with them that our behavior reveals it is not a core value, not one of the most important values. And the fruit of that behavior will be bad fruit. Another way to think of this is to look at each of our core beliefs and answer what kind of behavior and action would be logically expected from that belief, and then ask if our behavior matches that answer and are we getting the results we anticipated.

24. Covenant: *"For this is My blood of the new covenant, which is shed for many for the remission of sins."* (Matthew 26:28). *"Likewise He also took the cup after supper, saying, 'This cup is the new covenant in my blood which is shed for you.'"* (Luke 22:22). *" . . .and we have such trust through Christ toward God. Not that we are sufficient of ourselves to think of anything as being from ourselves, but our sufficiency is from God, who also made us sufficient as ministers of the new covenant, not of the letter but of the Spirit; for the letter kills, but the Spirit gives life."* (2 Corinthians 3:4-6).

It is often pointed out that Judaism and Christianity are each covenant traditions or religions that began with Adam and Eve, Noah, and Abraham (Genesis 3:6, Genesis 9:9, Genesis 12:1-3). Jesus was the *"mediator of a new covenant"* (Hebrews 12:24). The Old Covenant and New Covenant are now recently being called the Old and New Testaments. A covenant is a binding contract or agreement between two entities that binds them together with certain promises and expectations by each entity. A covenant between God and humans is generated by God for both the blessings and the wellbeing of the human. Humans receive and commit to the covenant by living faithfully to the agreements and obligations promised. God does not break His covenants but unfortunately we do.

Remember: We are a covenant people in a covenantal relationship with God and each other. God is clear about His promises and rewards for us and His expectations of us. We only need to obey the covenant.

25. Creation: *"In the beginning God made heaven and earth."* (Genesis 1:1).

Creation is essentially the thoughts and actions of God whereby He created all substance that was outside of Himself. *"In the beginning God created the heavens and the earth."* (Genesis 1:1). It is important to note that Father, Son, and Holy Spirit were all active in the Creation. (Genesis 1:2; John 1:1-3; Colossians 1:15-16; Hebrews 1:2; 11:3). One of the great mysteries of life and science is how something was created out of nothing. Clearly there are mysteries that will always be mysteries. One of the reasons we say God is both knowable and unknown. Basic questions we might ask are: Why did God create the universe? What was His intention? What was to be the relationship between God and humans? Will there be an end to creation? Is God still creating?

Remember: God created each one of us. God wants a relationship with each one of us. God has made promises and required expectations from each one of us. God has a purpose for each one of us. God is still actively involved in creation.

26. Creeds and Councils: *"Now the apostles and elders came together to consider this matter."* (Acts 15:6) The Jerusalem Council. *"Then it pleased the apostles and elders, with the whole church, to send chosen men of their own company to Antioch with Paul and Barnabas, namely Judas who was also named Barsabas, and Silas, leading men among the brethren."* (Acts 15:22).

After the New Testament Jerusalem Council there have been seven Ecumenical Councils. These were Councils that represented the entire world-wide, universal Christian Church known then as the One, Holy, Catholic, and Apostolic Church called simply the Catholic Church. All the Councils and Creeds occurred in the first six centuries before the schism between West and East in 1054. The Councils were deliberations determining what was authentic Christianity and what was counterfeit Christianity. The three creeds that came out of those Councils are the Apostles' Creed, The Nicene Creed, and the Athanasian Creed. Creed simply means "belief." In other words, the three Creeds state what the Church believes and teaches and therefore had and have authority. The authority of the Councils and the Three Creeds is derived from the fact that it was and is the Holy Spirit who was directing the Early Church and is directing the Christian Church today. The Bishops and representatives to the Ecumenical Councils and who developed the Creeds were prayerfully and faithfully guiding the Church and preserving the Faith *"once delivered to the saints."* They also lived very close to the Early Church. The Councils and Creeds were and should still be used as a polemic (that is defining true doctrine and declaring false doctrine) and as a teaching tool and in worship. The Nicene Creed and Apostles' Creed is used in worship today in the five largest denominations.

Remember: The Creeds and the Councils do not have the authority of the Bible but they do have authority to guide us in right doctrine and are worthy to be studied, believed, taught, and used in worship.

27. Cross of Christ: *"Therefore we also, since we are surrounded by so great a cloud of witnesses, let us lay aside every weight and the sin which so easily ensnares us, and let us run with endurance the race that is set before us, looking unto Jesus, the author and finisher of our faith, who for the joy that was set before Him endured the cross, despising the shame, and has sat down at the right hand of the throne of God."* (Hebrews 12:1-2).

Crucifixion on a stake or tree was a punishment practiced by the Romans which they had learned from other cultures. It was reserved for slaves and foreigners but not for Roman citizens. The Jews executed by stoning (Leviticus 20:2; Deuteronomy 13:10; 17:5). Dead bodies were sometimes hanged to the accursed tree, which was for the Jews a terrible symbol of shame (Deuteronomy 21:23). The cross in the New Testament also had practical aspects that are important. One is the horrible suffering involved in the brutality preceding the crucifixion and the actual death on the cross (Hebrews 2:9; 1 Peter 4:13). Another was the shame (Hebrews 12:4; 13:13). Making the condemned carry the cross to the place of crucifixion further emphasized the shame (Mark 15:21; Matthew 27:32; Luke 23:26;

John 19:17). For a Jew to be hanged on a tree was a curse, and Jesus was thus publicly disgraced in His crucifixion. At this time almost all the believers were Jews. After the resurrection, for a believer, the cross became the symbol of Christ's love for mankind (Galatians 3:13). The Gospel of Christ came to be called the Word of the Cross, or the Way of the Cross. Christians were often called people of the Way. (Ephesians 3:18–19). The Cross became the center of Paul's preaching (1 Corinthians 1:18). The weakness of the cross became the demonstration of the divine love (1 Corinthians 2:2; 2 Corinthians 13:4; 1 Corinthians 1:24–25). When Jesus says, *"And he who does not take his cross and follow after Me is not worthy of Me"* (Matthew 10:38), He means we are to love as He loved and walk as He walked. *To understand the Atoning sacrifice of Jesus on the Cross, see Sacrifice of Christ.*

Remember: The action and meaning of the Cross of Jesus is central to Christian faith and practice. One primary meaning is that the mystery of the Cross was a means of atonement for our sins bringing forgiveness and new life for us by the one, unique sacrifice of Jesus. A second meaning is the profound expression of God's love and Jesus' love for us. Thirdly, it is a dramatic presentation of how we are to live in the world.

[D] **28. Deacon:** *"Paul and Timothy, bondservants of Jesus Christ. To all the saints in Christ Jesus who are in Philippi with the bishops and deacons."* (Philippians 1:1).

The choosing of deacons is first mentioned in Acts 6:1-6. The Greek word simply means "to serve." In other words a "servant". The word elder came from our Jewish heritage but the word deacon came out of the culture. We are to be servants of Christ (John 12:26) who Himself was a servant (Romans 15:8: Galatians 2:17). Jesus commanded us to serve as He served (Mark 9:35; 10:43; 2 Corinthians 3:6; 11:23; Colossians 1:7). The first seven deacons were ordained by the apostles to deal with practical affairs of the Church such as the collection of offerings and the distribution of food and clothing to the poor. Elders were teachers, pastors, and evangelists. It is certain that women were ordained deacons (Romans 16:1). 1 Timothy 3:11 describes an order of women deacons. In some denominations deacons are preparation for becoming elders.

Remember: The three orders of clergy (Bishops, elders, and deacons) are equal in value of service to the Kingdom of God. It is simply a matter of different giftedness and calling.

29. Death: (Jesus said) *"Most assuredly, I say to you, he who hears My word and believes in Him who sent Me has everlasting life, and shall not come into judgment but has passed from death into life." "Most assuredly, I say to you, if anyone keeps My word he shall never see death."* (John 5:24; 8:51). *"Therefore, as through one man's offense judgment came to all men, resulting in condemnation, even so through one Man's righteous act the free gift came to all men, resulting in justification of life. For as by one man's disobedience many were made sinners, so also by one Man's obedience many will be made righteous."* (Romans 5:18-19). *" . . .but has now been revealed by the appearing of our Savior Jesus Christ who has abolished death and* *brought life and immortality to light through the gospel."* (2 Timothy 1:10).

Why do we die? Both the Old Testament and the New Testament assert with great clarity that believers are destined and meant to enjoy eternal or everlasting life. It was not God's intention that we should die. God was not the author of death. This truth is explicitly implied in the biblical account of the Fall of Adam and Eve due to the seduction by Satan (Genesis 3:19). In the New Testament Paul states this when he says, *"As sin came into the world through one man, and death through sin, and so death spread to all men because all men sinned . . ."* (Romans 5:12). The overarching concept in the New Testament is that humans are in bondage to sin and death. We live in separation from God. The good news is that sin and death have been conquered because of Christ. It was Christ's death that destroyed the power of the Evil One/Satan/Devil who is the lord of death (Hebrews 2:14-15). Christ's death brought immortality to us (2 Timothy 1:10). Our mortal bodies shall die but we are not separated from Christ (2 Corinthians 5:6; Philippians 1:20-21). Death cannot separate us from the love of God in Christ Jesus (Romans 8:38-39). Death, the last enemy has been destroyed (1 Corinthians 15:26). Believers in Christ will not see death (John 8:51-52).

Remember: We have all sinned. We will all die physically. However, we are all raised spiritually with a new body to everlasting life.

30. Denomination: In the New Testament, each local church saw itself as a part of the larger Church and accountable to it; first to the apostles and then to a larger representative body. A local church that is without higher accountability is not a New Testament church. Most local churches in the world belong to a larger community of churches. The connectedness is accomplished because of common denominators, usually theological and functional, (Doctrine and Discipline) and thus are called *denominations*. Even local churches who decry denominationalism many times belong to a structure-connected community. Our separation into different groups is more than regrettable, it is shameful.

Remember: The Early Church affirmed that we are believers and are a part "One, Holy, Catholic, Apostolic Church."

31. Demons: *"Then His fame went throughout all Syria; and they brought to Him all sick people who were afflicted with various diseases and torments, and those who were demon-possessed, epileptics, paralytics; and He healed them."* (Matthew 4:24). *"So they went out and preached that people should repent. And they cast out many demons, and anointed with oil many who were sick, and healed them."* (Mark 5:12-13).

Perhaps one of the most difficult aspects of reality to accept is that demons exist. However, if we accept Jesus and the Scripture teaching that the Evil One/ Devil/Satan is real, which Jesus clearly did, then the next logical step is to accept that demons are real. Demons are under the control of the Evil One/ Devil/Satan. The Bible portrays Jesus in combat against Satan whose attempts were and are to destroy the Kingdom of God (Matthew 12:29). Demons are portrayed as possessing high intelligence, power, and a cunning will (Mark 1:24; 9:17-27). Demons recognize the authority and power of Christ and His power over them (Mark 1:25; 3:11-12; 9:25). Jesus gave authority to the Twelve and the disciples to exorcise demons (Luke 9:1; 10:17). Exorcism, the ministry of expelling demons, is a ministry that is still necessary and is still practiced, especially in the Roman Catholic Church and the Orthodox Catholic Church. These two denominations have priests designated and trained to recognize and combat this expression of evil.

Remember: Though demons and their destructiveness are real, for one who is "in Christ", they are not to be feared. *See Devil.*

32. Devil/Evil One/Satan: *"Then Jesus, being filled with the Holy Spirit, returned from the Jordan and was led by the Spirit into the wilderness, being tempted forty days by the devil. And in those days He ate nothing, and afterward when they had ended, He was hungry. And the devil said to Him . . ."* (Luke 4:1-3). *"But Peter said, 'Ananias, why has Satan filled your heart to lie to the Holy Spirit . . .?'"* (Acts 5:3). Jesus said, *"But deliver us from the evil one."* (Matthew 6:13, Luke 11:4). Jesus said, *"I do not pray that you should take them out of the world, but that you should keep them from the evil one."* (John 17:15).

Jesus recognized the reality of the Evil One (Matthew 6:13: John 17:15). The literal meaning of the word is that of an accuser, a slanderer, a liar, and a maligner.

It is one of the names of Satan/Devil. In Scripture, the evil one is portrayed as serving several functions in the world against God and man. He accuses God to man (Genesis 3); he afflicts people with physical suffering (Acts 10:38); he tempts people to do evil (Ephesians 4:27; 6:11); he lays snares for people (1 Timothy 3:7); he seeks to devour people (1 Peter 5:8); he takes us captive (2 Timothy 2:26); and he deceives people (Ephesians 2:2). Jesus identified Judas with the Devil (John 6:70; 13:2). Believers are warned not to have pride as the Devil does (1 Timothy 3:6). The Devil's final end is the lake of fire (Matthew 25:41; Revelation 20:10). The good news is that if believers will only resist him, he will flee (James 4:7). The reason he will flee is that Christ, through His death, has won the victory over the devil (Hebrews 2:14). The Bible uses several names to describe this reality. Besides Devil, we see Satan, Evil One, the Tempter, the Father of lies, etc.

Remember: The Evil One is real and we should take evil seriously. However, when we live "in Christ" we are not afraid because we are secure. Christ has defeated the Evil One and we are assured of the final victory.

33. Disciple/Brother: *"Now when evening had come, there came a rich man from Arimathea, named Joseph, who himself had become a disciple of Jesus. The man went to Pilate and asked for the body of Jesus. Then Pilate commanded the body be given to him."* (Matthew 27:57-58). *"Then the word of God spread, and the number of the disciples multiplied greatly in Jerusalem, and a great many of the priests were obedient to the faith."* (Acts 6:7).

The word in the New Testament that is translated as "disciple" can also be translated as "brother" The terms are synonymous (Acts 18:27). The word can mean a pupil or student of a teacher or elder. In this case Jesus was the "teacher", the rabbi. The name generally became identified as someone who was a follower of Jesus, a Christian (Acts 14:21). Until recently it was common to call a fellow Christian "brother so-and-so or sister so-and-so" as an expression of affection and love for one another.

Remember: As followers of Jesus we are meant to have a special affection and love for our fellow disciples, followers of Jesus the Christ, our brothers and sisters.

34. Discipline: *"Do you not know that those who run in a race all run, but one receives the prize? Run in such a way that you may obtain it. And everyone who competes for the prize is temperate in all things. Now they do it to obtain a perishable crown, but we for an imperishable crown. Therefore I run thus; not with uncertainty. Thus not as one who beats the air. But I discipline my body and bring it to subjection, lest, when I have preached to others, I myself should become disqualified."* (1 Corinthians 9:24-27).

Two words that have been primary words in the history of the Christian Church are the words Doctrine and Discipline. Both are absolutely essential components of the life of the Christian and of the Church (Hebrews 12:7-11; 13:17; John 14:15-17). The Reverend John Wesley said, *"Better forty members should be lost than our discipline lost. Be exact in every point of discipline. Keep the rules and they will keep you."* Discipline is not a negative word. Discipline is a methodical approach that is a Methodist/Christian approach to achieving determined goals. Webster describes *strict* as "exact, accurate, precise, not loose or vague," and *discipline* meaning "training that develops self-control, character, or orderliness and efficiency; a system of rules, as for a church or monastic order." Training in any work, profession, or sport involves "strict discipline." A variety of words are integrally connected to being "disciplined". Words like obedient, self-controlled, commitment to recognized and accepted authority, commitment to the rules, self-control, and self-motivation. One thing is certain and that is without those ingredients goals are never achieved, whether personal or in the Kingdom of God.

Remember: To achieve "holiness of heart and life" whose product is happiness requires discipline. It is through discipline that we achieve desired goals and fully experience the benefits of the Christian life.

[E] **35. Elder:** *"And when they had preached the gospel to that city and made many disciples, they returned to Lystra, Iconium, and Antioch, strengthening the souls of the disciples, exhorting them to continue in the faith, and saying, 'We must through many tribulations enter the kingdom of God.' So when they had appointed elders in every church, and prayed with fasting, they commended them to the Lord in whom they had believed."* (Acts 14:21-23).

In the Old Testament God describes Himself as the Shepherd of Israel (Psalm 80:1). Prophets, priests, and elders were to perform as God's under-shepherds to the people. In the New Testament, Jesus is the Good Shepherd (John 10:11-30) and the Chief Shepherd (1 Peter 5:4). Peter describes his role as an "elder" (shepherd) under Jesus (1 Peter 5:4). The writings of Timothy, Titus, and Peter describe the work and the qualification of elders. Basically there are teachers and pastors, sometimes both of these in combination and some are ruling/leading elders. Some are "sent out" as evangelists or missionaries. It is all about giftedness, calling, and the blessing and appointment by the Church.

Remember: It may be an oversimplification but helpful to see the bishops (Elders/Presbyters) as overseers of doctrine and discipline in both clergy and laity, and elders as preachers, teachers, and or pastors (shepherds), protectors of the people, or evangelists. All with special emphasis on Word, Sacrament, and Mission. And deacons have responsibility and authority over all the practical matters of the Church. It is all about giftedness, calling, and appointment by the Church proper.

36. Eternal Life: *"Jesus answered, 'For God so loved the world that He gave His only begotten Son, that whoever believes in Him should not perish but have everlasting life.'"* (John 3:16). *"Therefore we do not lose heart. Even though our outward man is perishing, yet the inward man is being renewed day by day. For our light affliction, which is but for a moment, is working for us a far more exceeding and eternal weight of glory, while we do not look at the things which are seen, but at the things* *which are not seen, For the things which are seen are temporary, but the things which are not seen are eternal."* (2 Corinthians 4:16-18).

The word *eternal,* as it is used particularly in the New Testament, has several variations of meaning. However, the predominant meaning is that of a person or a thing the nature of which is endless. For example, God is endless (Romans 16:26); His power is endless (1 Timothy 6:16); and His Glory is endless (1 Peter 5:10). The Holy Spirit is endless (Hebrews 9:14). The salvation given by Jesus is endless (Hebrew 9:12). The future reign of Jesus is endless (2 Peter 1:11; Luke 1:33). Vastly important, the life that is given to us by Jesus Christ is endless (John 3:16). Paul described our resurrection as endless (2 Corinthians 5:1). One of the truly beautiful passages on this endless/eternal life given by Jesus is John 10:28 and 30, where we hear Jesus say to us, *"And I give them eternal life, and they shall never perish; neither shall anyone snatch them out of My hand. I and My Father are one."* The eternal life that is given to us by Jesus begins here and now and lasts eternally. In that sense eternal life begins here and now with our justification, regeneration, and sanctification, our holiness in Christ. In stating that *"I and My Father are one,"* Jesus was proclaiming that the promise in John 10:28 is given both by Jesus and by God. We can be confident that the life given now by Jesus is endless/eternal and we are assured of immortality.

Remember: God and Jesus keep promises. God and Jesus have promised us eternal life.

37. Eucharist: *"Then Jesus said to them, 'For the bread of God is He who comes down from heaven and gives life to the world. . . . Most assuredly I say to you, He who believes in Me has everlasting life. I am the bread of life . . . Most assuredly, I say to you, unless you eat the flesh of the Son of Man and drink His blood, you have no life in you. Whoever eats My flesh and drinks My blood has eternal life, and I will raise him up on the last day."* (John 6:33, 47, 48, 51, 53, 54).

Also called the Lord's Supper, Holy Communion, the Breaking of Bread, the Mass, etc. The Greek word *eucharistein* (eulogein) literally means "thanksgiving." In the Old Testament the root of the word is found multiple times and always refers to thankfulness, praise, blessing, or confession. In the New Testament, the word is used as a verb thirty-nine times and as a noun fifteen times. It always means "thankfulness or gratitude." The intention is our complete thankfulness and gratitude to God for Christ (2 Corinthians 2:14). Our thankfulness is expressed in our words and deeds, although these can never in any way equal our indebtedness to God for what has been done for us in Christ Jesus. Thankfulness or gratitude is the first primary motive of the Christian life (Matthew 10:8; 18:32; 1 Corinthians 6:20; Ephesians 4:32). Gratitude is the fuel of the heart. When Jesus was with His disciples at the Last Supper, He followed the usual Jewish customs of piety. Hence the words *thanksgiving* and *blessing* in this context. St. Ignatius was using the actual word *thanksgiving* as the formal word for the sacrament as early as A.D. 115. The names in the New Testament were the breaking of bread (Acts 20:7) and the Lord's Supper (1 Corinthians 11:20), which included a real meal. It appears as though by the year A.D. 100. the real meal had been separated from the sacramental meaning. It is important to remember that the bread blessing and the cup blessing were separated by an entire meal. The promise Jesus made to the disciples in that original Lord's Supper was that in the breaking of the bread He would be there with them. The promise Jesus made in the wine is that He would be with them as their Savior and He was initiating a New Covenant through His death.

What is the meaning of this sacrament commanded by Jesus? The first meaning is that the primary gift in this sacrament of thanksgiving is the real presence of our Lord Jesus Christ. The real meaning of 1 Corinthians 16:22 is "Our Lord has come" or "Our Lord is here." The "thanksgiving" is the promise that Jesus made that He will come and be with His beloved. Christ Himself will be present at the Eucharist to meet those seeking forgiveness and desiring to love and obey Him. Secondly, the Eucharist proclaims the power of the Cross of Christ. It proclaims the initiation of the New Covenant and the attending promises that go with it. Thirdly, the Eucharist reminds us of the future promise where we will be with Jesus in Paradise. Fourthly, the Eucharist binds all of us Christians together in sacrificial love for each other because of the love of Christ. Fifthly, the Eucharist reminds us of the sacrificial love of Christ and His love for each of us. And sixthly, it is where we retake our oath of love and loyalty to our only Lord and savior, Jesus our Christ. We believe in the Real Presence at Holy

Communion. God the Father, Jesus the Son, and the Holy Spirit are all present.

Remember: At the Holy Communion we believe in the Real Presence of Christ and can experience the love, forgiveness, healing, new life, and the unsurpassed joy of being in the presence of the Trinity and being touched, healed, and restored by them. *See Sacrifice.*

38. Evil/Evildoer: *"So Jesus said, 'Are you also without understanding? But those things which proceed out of the mouth come from the heart, and they defile a man. For out of the heart proceed evil thoughts, murders, adulteries, fornications, thefts, false witness, blasphemies. These are the things that defile a man . . .'"* (Matthew 15:17-20). *"For from within, out of the heart proceed evil thoughts, adulteries, fornications, murders, thefts, covertness, wickedness, deceit, lewdness, an evil eye, blasphemy, pride, foolishness. All these evil things come from within and defile."* (Mark 7:21-23).

As an overarching concept it means that which is destructive, malicious, and injurious. It is that which is antithetical to goodness and its purpose seeks to destroy goodness. In the New Testament, *evil* refers to persons who are ethically or morally evil (Matthew 21:41; 24:48; Philippians 3:2). It can also refer to character or deeds that are evil (Mark 7:21; John 18:23; Romans 1:30; 1 Corinthians 13:4). It is described as wickedness, depravity, or malignity (Acts 8:22; Romans 1:29). In James 1:21, it is described as maliciousness. Satan is described as the "evil one" (Matthew 5:37; 6:13; 13:19, 38). Some human beings are evil (Matthew 5:45;

Luke 6:35; 1 Corinthians 5:13). Overcoming evil begins with us. The very first endeavor we as individuals need to take is to properly order our lives so that we are living in righteousness and holiness. That goal cannot be achieved without first recognizing the propensity for sin and evil in our own hearts. It is extremely difficult for most people to accomplish that goal without being part of a community that teaches and practices holiness of heart and life.

Remember: Evil is real and is maliciously destructive. Living in Christ gives us the power over evil. In this world it is a lifetime battle.

[F] **39. Forgiveness**: *"He has delivered us from the power of darkness and conveyed us into the kingdom of the Son of His love, in whom we have redemption through His blood, the forgiveness of sins."* (Colossians 1:13-14). *"If we confess our sins, He is faithful and just to forgive us our sins and to cleanse us from all unrighteousness."* (1 John 1:9).

God is a Holy God and demands holiness from His people (Leviticus 11:44–45; 1 Peter 1:16). Mankind's failure to keep God's commandments and expectations by sinning demands God's punishment. Love demands justice. Because of God's grace and mercy He has decided to forgive us and offer a new opportunity of love and obedience. Forgiveness is the putting away and the cancelation of the injury caused by our sin. The result is our being forgiven. Forgiveness can relate to the cancelation of debts (Matthew 6:12; 18:27, 32), or to the remission of sins (Matthew 9:2, 5, 6; 12:31, 32; Acts 8:22; Romans 4:7;

James 5:15; 1 John 1:9; 2:12). In the Old Testament, an act of atoning sacrifice was associated with forgiveness (Leviticus 4:20, 26). In the New Testament that atoning sacrifice was performed by Jesus when He became the sacrifice for our sins. Justification is that act whereby, because of the righteousness of Jesus and His sacrifice, we are pardoned and forgiven. The pardon is completely the gracious act of God and none of it is accomplished by any merit of ours. Forgiveness after justification is dependent upon our repentance and confession (Matthew 18:15–17; Luke 17:3). Humanity, having received this unmerited forgiveness, is expected to forgive others (Matthew 6:1–2, 14–15; Luke 17:3; Mark 11:25).

Remember: True repentance brings forgiveness from all our sins. Forgiveness brings peace.

40. Fruit of the Spirit: *"And this I pray, that your love may abound still more and more in knowledge and all discernment, that you may approve the things that are excellent, that you may be sincere and without offence till the day of Christ, being filled with fruits of righteousness which are by Jesus Christ, to the glory and praise of God."* (Philippians 1:9-11). *"But now having been set free from sin, and having become slaves to God, you have your fruit to holiness, and the end, everlasting life. For the wages of sin is death, but the gift of God is eternal life in Christ Jesus our Lord."* (Romans 6:22-23).

The reference to the fruit of righteousness is found in Galatians 5:22–23. The passage refers to the power of the Holy Spirit operating in people to bring us into a living union with Christ. (John 15:2–8, 16). Our union with Christ produces the fruit of the Spirit. The *fruit* is singular because it claims the unity of the character of Christ formed in us, that being love, joy, peace, longsuffering (patience), kindness, goodness, faithfulness, gentleness, and self-control. In other references, the fruits are plural signifying growing in grace, knowledge, and holiness.

Remember: We can do nothing good on our own. It is the power of the Holy Spirit living in us who will produce wonderful fruit.

[G] **41. Glorification:** *" . . .and when the Chief Shepherd appears, you will receive the crown of glory that does not fade away. Therefore humble yourselves under the mighty hand of God, that He may exalt you in good time. But may the God of all grace, who called us to His eternal glory by Christ Jesus, after you have suffered a while, perfect, establish, strengthen, and settle you. To Him be the glory and the dominion forever and ever. Amen."* (1 Peter 5:4, 6, 10).

The time when God acts we who have died in Christ will receive our renewed bodies (Romans 8:23). At that time "the perishable" will "clothe itself with the imperishable," and the mortal body will put on immortality (1 Corinthians 15:53). The last enemy, death, will be swallowed up in victory (1 Corinthians 15:26, 54).

Remember: That wonderful promised day is waiting for each and every one of us. The final blessing of our salvation.

42. Glory: *"And behold, an angel of the Lord stood before them, and the glory of the Lord shone around them, and they were greatly afraid. Then the angel said to them, 'Do not be afraid, for behold, I bring you good tidings of great joy which will be to all people. For there is born to you this day in the city of Davis a Savior, who is Christ the Lord.'"* (Luke 2:9-11). *"Jesus spoke these words, lifted up His eyes to heaven, and said; 'Father, the hour has come. Glorify your Son, that Your Son also may glorify You, as You have given Him authority over all flesh, that He should give eternal life to as many as You have given Him. And this is eternal life, that they may know You, the only true God, and Jesus Christ whom You have sent. I have glorified You on the earth. I have finished the work which You have given Me to do. And now, O Father, glorify Me together with Yourself, with the glory which I had with You before the world was.'"* (John 17:1-5).

This word like the word "God" is difficult to put in a short explanation. It was used in the Old Testament to point to the power, majesty, and loving-kindness of God, the very reality of God. It is in the respect that we see the reality of God's presence in the drowning of the Egyptians in the Red Sea. *"And in the morning you shall see the glory of the Lord."* (Exodus 16:7). The "glory of the Lord" denoted the powerful manifestation of God. In the New Testament the "glory of God" was revealed in the birth of Jesus (Luke 2:9). In other words, God's power and holiness was made manifest. The manifestation was present at the Transfiguration, where Peter, James, and John were present with Jesus, Moses, and Elijah (Matthew 1:1-8). Glory is the presence of that which is real and experiential yet mysterious and incomprehensible.

Remember: The God of Glory is power and holiness that evokes love, awe, humility, and obedience.

43. God: *"Jesus said to him, 'I am the way, the truth, and the life. No one comes to the Father except through Me. If you had known Me you would have known My Father also; and from now on you know Him and have seen Him.' Phillip said to Him, 'Lord, show us the Father, and it is sufficient for us.' Jesus said to him, 'Have I been with you so long, and yet you have not known Me, Phillip? He who has seen Me has seen the Father, so how can you say, "Show us the Father?" Do you not believe that I am in the Father and the Father in Me?'"* (John 14:6-10).

God is simply a word we use to try and describe the indescribable, the knowable yet unknowable, the Creator and Sustainer of all that exists. That is why in the Old Testament we read several names used to address and speak about God; Yahweh, Elohim, El Shaddai, Adoni, the name that cannot be spoken, and a multitude of other phrases and descriptions of the person and nature of this supernatural Essence beyond us but actively living in us and in the world. Perhaps the most personal, loving, and heartwarming name given to God is the one used by Jesus, Abba (Mark 14:36). It is the name a child would use to address a father and expresses the deep love and relationship between Jesus and God. Jesus taught us the Lord's Prayer which begins "Our Father." It is only because of the love of God in Christ and our relationship with Jesus and the Holy Spirit that we can address God as "Our Father." Whatever word we use or do not use, the word is meant to express a Presence outside of human existence that is a power of creation and love beyond our human comprehension.

Remember: God in all His power and holiness desires the kind of loving and obedient relationship with us where we can say "Our father."

44. Godhead: *"For the wrath of God is revealed from heaven against all ungodliness and unrighteousness of men, who suppress the truth in unrighteousness. For since the creation of the world His invisible attributes are clearly seen, being understood by things that are made, even His eternal power and Godhead, so that they are without excuse."* (Romans 1:18, 19, 20). *"For in Him dwells all the fullness of the Godhead bodily."* (Colossians 2:9).

In 2 Peter 1:3, the word *divine* is used to describe the power and might of God. The derivation of the word *divine* is from the same Greek word for God. Verse 4 describes God's nature. God's Peter says here that God's "divine power" has been given through Jesus so that we might be "partakers of the divine nature." In Acts 17:29, it is used as a noun to denote the "Godhead," the One True God. It also represents the Trinity, the Three-in-One who constitutes the Trinity—Father, Son, and Holy Spirit.

Remember: There are three distinct and separate persons, co-equal and of one substance.

45. Grace: *"And the Word became flesh and dwelt among us, and we beheld His glory, the glory as of the only begotten of the Father, full of grace and truth. And of His fullness we have all received, and grace for grace. For the law was given through Moses, but grace and truth came through Jesus Christ."* (John 1:14-16). *"Grace to you and peace from God our Father and the Lord Jesus Christ. Blessed be the God and Father of our Lord Jesus Christ, who has blessed us with every spiritual blessing in the heavenly places in Christ, just as He chose us in Him before the foundation of the world, that we should be holy and without blame before Him in love, having predestined us to adoption as sons by Jesus Christ to Himself, according to the good pleasure of His will, to the praise of the glory of His grace, by which He made us acceptable in the Beloved."* (Ephesians 1:3-6).

The concept of grace is fundamental to both the Old Testament and New Testament. The Bible is the story of the grace of God reaching out to humanity. We hear in Genesis 6:8 that *"Noah found grace in the eyes of the Lord."* God's choosing Israel was totally undeserved by Israel (Deuteronomy 7:7–8, 14–18; 9:4–6). The Prophets' main message was to call back a backsliding people to God's grace (Isaiah 43:2–15; Jeremiah 18:8–11; Ezekiel 16). In the Old Testament the grace is associated with a covenant, and that covenant is the Law. In the New Testament, the New Covenant fulfills the Old Covenant. *"For in Him [Jesus] dwells the fullness of the Godhead bodily"* (Colossians 2:9). God's grace is now made manifest in Jesus the Christ. The grace of God offering salvation is now found in Jesus and is available to all who believe in Him. We now can be justified in Jesus (Romans 3:21–24). This grace is a free gift that cannot be earned (Ephesians 2:4–9; Romans 3:24; 11:6; 2 Timothy 1:9). It is grace itself that causes us to turn to God (Acts 5:31; 2:18; 16:14; Hebrews 6:6). Faith is a free gift of grace (Ephesians 1:19; Philippians 1:29). All we receive is by grace, whether our justification (Romans 5:2; 1 Peter 2:10) or our sanctification (1 Thessalonians 5:23). Therefore, from beginning to end the grace of God is activated through the Holy Spirit, whose function is the work of grace in the human heart.

Remember: Grace is such an important gift of God in Christian theology we have included *The Ten Doctrines of Grace* from Catechism 1, The Methodist Episcopal Church: New York; Hunt and Eaton. 1884. P.30.

- I. I believe that all mankind are sinners.
- II. I believe that God the Father loves all people and hates sin.
- III. I believe that Jesus Christ died for all to make possible their salvation from sin, and to make sure the salvation of all who believe in Him.
- IV. I believe that the Holy Spirit is given to all to enlighten and to incline them to repent of their sins and to believe in the Lord Jesus Christ.
- V. I believe that all who repent of their sins and believe in the Lord Jesus Christ receive the forgiveness of sin. [This is justification]
- VI. I believe that all who receive the forgiveness of sin are at the same time made new creatures in Christ Jesus. [This is regeneration]

VII. I believe that all who are made new creatures in Christ Jesus are accepted as children of God. [This is adoption]

VIII. I believe that all who are accepted as children of God may receive the inward assurance of the Holy Spirit to that fact. [This is the witness of the Spirit]

IX. I believe that all who truly desire and seek it, may love God with all their heart and soul, and mind and strength, and their neighbors as themselves. [This is entire sanctification]

X. I believe that all who persevere to the end, and only those, shall be saved in heaven forever. [This is the true final perseverance]

46. Great Commandments: *"You are My friends if you do whatever I command you. No longer do I call you servants, for a servant does not know what his master is doing; but I have called you friends, for all things that I heard from My Father I have made known to you. You did not choose Me, but I chose you and appointed you that you should go and bear fruit, and that fruit should remain, that whatever you ask the Father in My name He may give you. These things I command you. That you love one another."* (John 15:14-17).

In Mark 12:30–31, Jesus shares a two-part answer to a question about what is the greatest commandment. He says that above all else we are called to love the Trinity (God the Father; Jesus, God's Son; and God the Holy Spirit) with everything we have because our life depends on our loving God with all our heart, soul, mind, and strength. In part two of His answer, He says that loving one another as much as we love ourselves is just as important as loving God with everything we have. Later in John 13:34, Jesus expands on the Great Commandment with what is referred to as the New Commandment. Here Jesus further sharpens God's call to love our neighbor by calling us to not just love others as much as we love ourselves, but to love them as much as Christ loves us.

Remember: First, we always keep before us the goal of love of God and neighbor. And then we pray fervently, diligently in the Spirit, seeking the help of our Christian community to understand what love is.

47. Great Commission: *"And He said to them . . . But you shall receive power when the Holy Spirit has come upon you; and you shall be witnesses to Me in Jerusalem, and in all Judea and Samaria, and to the end of the earth."* (Acts 1:7-8). *"For 'whoever calls on the name of the Lord shall be saved.' How then shall they call on Him in whom they have not believed? And how shall they believe in Him of whom they have not heard? And how shall they hear without a preacher? And how shall they preach unless they are sent?"* (Romans 10:13-15).

One of the last instructions Jesus told His followers (and therefore one of the most important things He told them) was to *"Go . . . and make disciples of all the nations, baptizing them in the name of the Father and of the Son and of the Holy Spirit, teaching them to observe all things that I have commanded you."* (Matthew 28:19–20). This is known as the Great Commission—our mandate to share the Good News of Jesus Christ with those who are not yet believers so they can come to faith in Christ. Our mandate continues as the new believers are baptized and as we help them become true disciples (mature followers of Jesus), teaching them everything they need to know and experience so they can become Kingdom People experiencing Kingdom living as a way of life.

Remember: Gratitude for what God in Christ has done for us compels us to want to introduce people to Jesus in order for them to become like Him and participate in the happiness of holiness.

[H] **48. Heaven:** *"For our citizenship is in heaven, from which we also eagerly wait for the Savior. The Lord Jesus Christ, who will transform our lowly body that it may be conformed to His glorious body, according to the working by which He is able even to subdue all things to Himself. Therefore, my beloved and longed-for brethren, my joy and crown, so stand fast in the Lord, beloved."* (Philippians 3:20-21). Jesus said, *"Let not your heart be troubled; believe in God, believe also in Me. In My Father's house are many mansions; if it were not so, I would have told you. I go to prepare a place for you. And if I go and prepare a place for you, I will come again and receive you to Myself; that where I am you may be also."* (John 14:1-4).

Jesus was the first person in this world to rise eternally from the dead (Acts 26:23). Jesus promised to raise those who loved and obeyed Him (1 Corinthians 15:20-23; Philippians 3:20-21). In reality, Jesus is going to raise everyone from the dead, some to eternal life and some to eternal punishment. Paul gives a wonderful promise in 1 Corinthians 15:45-54 of our transfiguration. We will receive a body that is eternal and immortal. At the transfiguration of Jesus both Moses and Elijah were present and recognizable (Matthew 17:3-4). So will we be recognizable at our resurrection. And so will be the people we love. Heaven is basically God's dwelling place for us (John 14:2). Heaven is where God will make Himself fully known to us and where we will be His people forever (Revelation 21:3).

Remember: We do not know what heaven is really like, it is simply that we want to go there.

49. Hell: (Jesus said) *"When the Son of Man comes in His glory, and all the holy angels with Him, then He will sit on the throne of His glory . . . And these will go away into everlasting punishment, but the righteous into eternal life."* (Matthew 25:31, 46). *"And I say to you, My friends, do not be afraid of those who kill the body, and after that have no more that they can do. But I will show you whom you should fear. Fear Him, after he has killed, has power to cast into hell; yes, I say to you, fear Him."* (Luke 12:5-6).

Jesus says clearly in Matthew 25:31-46 that there will be a judgment day. Some will live eternally with Him and some will be eternally punished (Revelation 20:14-15). We will be judged for what we have done in this life (Romans 2:6; Matthew 16:27; 2 Corinthians 5:10; Revelations 22:12). Some people think the love of God is so great that in the final analysis He will forgive all or give everyone an opportunity at the last moment to repent. This is simply not true. None of us want to think about judgment but it is a coming reality for each of us.

Remember: What is hell like? We really do not know for sure. What we do know is simply that we do not want to go there.

50. Holiness: *"And may the Lord make you increase and abound in love to one another and to all, just as we do to you, so that He may establish your hearts blameless in holiness before our God and Father at the coming of our Lord Jesus Christ with all His saints."* (1 Thessalonians 3:12-13). *"But you are a chosen generation, a royal priesthood, a holy nation, His own special people, that you may proclaim the praises of Him who called you out of darkness into His marvelous light."* (1 Peter:2:9).

A Holy People in Christ's Holy Church has always been the supreme goal of the Christian life and the Christian Church. God said, *"Be holy, for I am holy."* (Leviticus 11:44, 45; 19:2; 20:7). It is not a suggestion, it is a command. 1 Peter 1:16 quotes this, *"Be holy, for I am holy."* Hebrews 12:14 says, *"Pursue peace with all people, and holiness, without which no one will see the Lord."* We pray this thought every time we pray the Lord's Prayer, *"Hallowed (Holy) be your name."* It was especially the Hebrews 12:14 quote that convinced the Anglican priest Reverend John Wesley of the holiness mandate. It was the reason he said that God had raised up the people called Methodists and Rev. Wesley's emphasis changed the Christian world. We interpret holiness, sanctification, perfection, perfect love, and righteousness to mean nearly the same thing. In one basic broad sense they are interchangeable. Holiness is a life totally dedicated to union with God. It is a life whose whole desire is the love of God and the love of neighbor. It is a life desiring to be made in the image of Christ and walk as He walked. It is a life committed to loving and obeying Christ. It is Christ living in us, the perfect living in the imperfect. Holiness of heart and life does not free us from mistakes, ignorance, infirmities, or temptations but it assists us in becoming overcomers and to participate in Christ's holiness, to be "partakers of the divine nature." (2 Peter 1:3-4).

Remember: God in Christ calls each of us to be "A Holy People in Christ's Holy Church."

51. Holy Communion/ Holy Eucharist—See *Eucharist*.

52. Holy Spirit: *" . . .for the kingdom of God is not eating and drinking but righteousness and peace and joy in the Holy Spirit." (Romans 14:17). "And so we have the prophetic word confirmed, which you do well to heed as a light that shines in a dark place, until the day dawns and the morning star rises in your hearts; knowing this first, that no prophecy of Scripture is of any private interpretation, for prophecy never came by the will of man, but holy men of God spoke as they were moved by the Holy Spirit."* (2 Peter 1:19-21).

The Holy Spirit is the Spirit of God. The older Bible translations called Him the "Holy Ghost". The Spirit was with God from the beginning and is co-eternal with God. The Holy Spirit who was supremely active in the Old Testament also filled Jesus with the power to do His work, the work of God. Jesus has given us the Holy Spirit to do His work, and He made the Holy Spirit the Administrator of the Church—the Holy Spirit is in supreme charge. The Spirit is the One who convicts us of sin. The Spirit is the One who brings about our justification and sanctification. The Holy Spirit is one of the three Persons of the Trinity with whom we are meant to have a personal relationship and who is meant to be worshiped as we worship God and Jesus.

Remember: The Holy Spirit is a person that we are meant to know, love, and follow as we follow Jesus.

[I] **53. Idolatry:** *"If then you were raised with Christ, seek those things which are above, where Christ is, sitting at the right hand of God. Set your mind on things above, not on the things of the earth. For you died, and your life is hidden with Christ in God. When Christ who is our life appears, then you will appear with Him in glory. Therefore put to death your members which are on the earth; fornication, uncleanness, passion, evil desires, and covetousness, which is idolatry."* (Colossians 3:1-6). *"Now the works of the flesh are evident, which are: adultery, fornication, uncleanness, lewdness, idolatry, sorcery, hatred, contentions, jealousies, outbursts of wrath, selfish ambitions, dissensions, heresies, envy, murders, drunkenness, revelries, and the like: of which I tell you beforehand, just as I also told you in the past, that those who practice such things will not inherit the kingdom of God."* (Galatians 5:19-21).

Idolatry is the worship of any image or substance other than God (Matthew 6:19-24). It can be self, family, country, power, money, pleasure, or even some objects that would be considered good. We might belong to a church or a denomination that we rightly love. At the same time our love can become obsessive to the point that the church or the institution becomes more important than our love and obedience to the Kingdom of God.

Remember: We worship only the Trinity. If we have the right love and relationship with the Trinity we will have a loving and right relationship with ourselves, spouse, family, church, country, and world.

54. Incarnation: *"Now in the sixth month the angel Gabriel was sent by God to a city of Galilee named Nazareth, to a virgin betrothed to a man whose name was Joseph, of the house of David. The virgin's name was Mary. And having come in, the angel said to her, 'Rejoice, highly favored one, the Lord is with you; blessed are you among women.' But when she saw him, she was troubled at his saying, and considered what manner of greeting this was. Then the angel said to her, 'Do not be afraid, Mary, for you have found favor with God. And behold you will conceive in your womb and bring forth a Son, and shall call His name Jesus. He will be great, and will be called the Son of the Highest; and the Lord God will give Him the throne of His father David. And He will reign over the house of Jacob forever, and of His kingdom there will be no end.' Then Mary said to the angel, 'How can this be, since I do not know a man?' And the angel answered and said to her, 'The Holy Spirit will come upon you, and the power* *of the Highest will overshadow you; therefore, also, that Holy One who is to be born will be called the Son of God.'"* (Luke 1:26-35).

The Incarnation and the Resurrection are two primary dimensions of Christianity which separate us from all other religions or expressions of faith. The word incarnate substantially means *"entered into flesh"*. That is why John used the language *"The word became flesh and dwelt among us."* (John 1:14). The Incarnation occurred when the Son of God by the Holy Spirit entered into the womb of Mary. Thus we have the *"virgin birth"* (Isaiah 7:14; Matthew 1:16-25; Luke 1:27, 34-35; 2:5; Galatians 4:4). The essence of Jesus then is that in one real human person there is a wholly divine presence of God. The Church has always affirmed that Jesus was fully human and fully divine. Many times the Church has had to fight against false teachings that said either Jesus was not truly fully human or that Jesus was not truly fully divine. No wonder the Jews, and because of the crucifixion of Jesus the apostles and disciples, had a difficult time understanding or believing what had truly happened. It was the Resurrection that turned the world upside down and changed history forever and then the Incarnation was understood. *See The Two Natures of Jesus.*

Remember: The mystery of the Incarnation of Jesus proclaims that Jesus was a complete human being experiencing what we experience and dealing with all of the temptations and what it means to be human; hunger, exhaustion, pain, all of it. And yet He was sinless and by His life and death made a pathway for us. A pathway of forgiveness, new life, holiness, and eternal life.

[J] **55. Jesus:** *"Then Joseph, being aroused from sleep, did as the angel of the Lord commanded him and took to him his wife, and did not know her till she had brought forth her firstborn Son. And he called His name Jesus."* (Matthew 1:24-25).

Who was Jesus? Who is Jesus? The name Jesus is a transliteration of the Hebrew name Joshua, meaning "Jehovah (One of the names of God in the Old Testament) is salvation," or "the one who saves," or just "savior." The name was given by an angel to Joseph, the husband of Mary, Jesus' mother, prior to Jesus' birth (Matthew 1:21). The word Christ is a Greek word for "anointed." The Hebrew word for "anointed" is Messiah. Jesus was thus "The Anointed One," "the Christ," or "the long anticipated Messiah." It was not long before people referred to Jesus as Jesus Christ rather than Jesus *the* Christ. There are essentially three secular sources of importance concerning Jesus: Pliny (Epistles: 10:96), Tacitus (Annals: 15:44), and Suetonius (Lives: 24:4). These three date from the second century. The primary Jewish sources are Josephus (Antiquities: 18.3.3; 20.9.1) and the Talmud. What is universally agreed on from these sources is that Jesus lived, He gathered disciples around Him, He taught, and He performed miracles. It is agreed that He was condemned to crucifixion and death by Pontius Pilot. There are a number of non-biblical sources that are presumably but doubtfully written by Christians during the next three centuries. The stories are so fantastic as to not have little credibility although they are interesting to read. That leaves the four gospels, Matthew, Mark, Luke, and John, and the writings of Acts through Revelation as those that were decided to faithfully represent the life, death, and resurrection of Jesus and what that event meant. The cataclysmic event though was the Resurrection of Jesus. Jewish and Roman doctors would have certified His death as well as the testimony of the followers of Jesus who were witnesses at the crucifixion. It was the Resurrection of Jesus that changed His followers and eventually the world.

Remember: Jesus was God manifested in the real man Jesus who was and is our Savior and who lives and reigns at the right hand of God the Father. *Read The Apostles Creed and the Nicene Creed.*

56. Justification: *"For by grace you have been saved through faith, and that not of yourselves; it is the gift of God, not of works, lest anyone should boast."* (Ephesians 2:8–9). *"Therefore let it be known to you, brethren, that through this Man is preached to you the forgiveness of sins; and by Him everyone is justified from all things . . ."* (Acts 15:38-39).

"But to him who does not work but believes on Him who justifies the ungodly, his faith is accounted for righteousness." (Romans 4:5). The renewed teaching on justification by faith, which was in disuse, was the doctrine that initiated the Protestant Reformation. The essential understanding of justification is pardon—the forgiveness of our sins. Justification is the gracious

act of God who through the sacrifice of Christ (Atonement) showed us His mercy by forgiving our sins. When we are forgiven, God will never hold our previous sins against us. Justification does not mean we are instantly made righteous, sanctified, or holy; rather, that is the work of sanctification. Regeneration and sanctification begins at the moment we are justified, but it is a completely different work. Justification is what God has done for us through the sacrifice of Jesus on the cross. Sanctification is what happens within us as we cooperate with the Holy Spirit in our growth in holiness.

Remember: Justification is the gracious love and gift of forgiveness and pardon God has done for us in the Cross of Christ.

[K] **57. Kingdom of God**: *"Now after John was put in prison, Jesus came to Galilee preaching the gospel of the kingdom of God, and saying, 'The time is fulfilled, and the kingdom of God is at hand. Repent, and believe in the gospel.'"* (Mark 1:14). *"And Jesus answered and said to them . . . 'And the gospel of the kingdom will be peached in all the world as a witness to all the nations, and then the end will come.'"* (Matthew 24:14).

Two things are important to remember. One is that the Kingdom of God is the central message of Jesus. Second, the Kingdom of God is that place where God reigns both now and forever. It is God's Kingdom not ours. It is the place where God is in control, not us. It is the place where God rules in our hearts and minds and souls.

58. Kingdom Issues: Kingdom issues are the ones of primary importance in the Kingdom of God, as opposed to secondary or extraneous issues to the Kingdom of God. Here are five major Kingdom issue areas: (1) Our personal worship life, which involves our prayer life, fasting, Bible study, etc. (2) Our Church life, which involves our corporate worship, sacramental life, service, stewardship, etc. (3) Our biblical and theological essentials and our fidelity to them. (4) The conduct of our lives, the holiness of our hearts and lives, whether or not our behavior is matching our beliefs. (5) Our serving Christ in the world.

59. Kingdom Living: Kingdom living is essentially loving God with all our hearts, minds, souls, and strength, and loving our neighbors as ourselves. It is being filled with such a divine love that all our outward and inward desires are directed at expressing the love that is given to us by the power of the Holy Spirit. Kingdom Living is being one in union with the Trinity, having Christ living in our hearts, being formed in the image of Christ, and walking as He walked. It is having the power of the Holy Spirit teaching and leading us so we will serve Christ in the world. This applies to individuals as well as congregations. Kingdom living brings peace, purpose, and power for living to the fullest as we personally experience spiritual transformation. What this means in the real world of living, working, relationships, and faith is this: We can live at a higher level than we currently live. We can rise above troubles, despair, and opposition to deal with Kingdom issues in life. We can continue to grow in love and in knowledge that makes us more complete, mature human beings.

60. Kingdom People: People who live in the Kingdom of God. People who have committed themselves to the pursuit of holiness or complete sanctification. People for whom God rules their entire lives. People who are united with God: Father, Son, and Holy Spirit, formed in the image of Jesus Christ, taught and led by the Holy Spirit, and serving Christ in the world.

[L] **61. Law:** (Jesus said) *"Do not think that I came to destroy the Law or the Prophets. I did not come to destroy but to fulfill."* (Matthew 5:17). *"Owe to no one anything except to love one another, for he who loves another has fulfilled the law."* (Romans 13:8).

Innumerable books have been written explaining the Old Testament and the New Testament understanding of "law". In the Old Testament, theologians typically have divided the law into three categories: moral, civic, and ceremonial. Civic and ceremonial laws usually change within cultures or generations of time. <u>Moral laws do not change</u>. The moral laws of the Bible are eternal. The dietary, purity, and sacrificial laws were abolished with the coming of Jesus (Matthew 15:20; Mark 7:15-9; 1 Timothy 4:3-5; Hebrews 10:1-14). Civic laws have to do with how a community protects and governs itself. Clearly the Christian moral laws are meant to protect the innocent and punish evildoers within a compassionate and just society. The law is meant to convict us of sin and motivate us to repentance (Romans 3:20). The law is meant to guide us in holiness and morality so that we live under the law of Christ (Galatians 6:2). The law is our friend and helper.

Remember: The moral law is a guide and delight to those who desire obedience to Christ.

62. Legalism: *See Works*

63. Love of God and Neighbor: *See Great Commandment*

[M] **64. Martyr**: *"And when the blood of Your martyr Stephen was shed, I also was standing by consenting to his death, and guarding the clothes of those who were killing him."* (Acts 22:20). *"Therefore we also, since we are surrounded by so great a cloud of witnesses, let us lay aside every weight, and the sin which so easily ensnares us, and let us run with swift endurance the race that is set before us, looking unto Jesus, the author and finisher of our faith, who for the joy that was set before Him endured the cross, despising the shame, and has sat down at the right hand of the throne of God."* (Hebrews 12:1-2).

The Greek word actually means "witness" and is found consistently throughout the New Testament. It can either mean someone who has testified to the faith because of their witness to the faith or someone who by word or deed has been killed. It is more often today used as referring to those people who have been or are being murdered because of their Christian faith. It is a sobering reality that every year numerous Christians are being murdered in countries around the world simply because they testify to Jesus as Lord.

Remember: Every believer is a witness every moment by what we say and what we do. Even today that witness may require our life.

65. Mary Mother of Jesus: *See Incarnation and The Magnificat* (A hymn of praise to God by Mary) (Luke 1:46-56).

Old Testament prophecies have been ascribed to Mary (Genesis 3:15, Isaiah 7:14, Jeremiah 31:22, and Micah 5:2-23). In the New Testament, Matthew says little about Mary except for stressing that she is a virgin (Matthew 1:18-25). Until recently, most Christians accepted the Virgin Birth without question. Christians who believe in the historical Church's teaching still do believe in the Virgin Birth. Luke has more to say in relating her relationship with Elizabeth, her magnificent song to God and her trips with Jesus (Luke 1:26-2:51). John depicts Mary at the foot of the Cross (John 19:25-27). Jesus loved His mother and entrusted Mary and John to each other. It is a loving, tender, and tragic scene in that Mary who gave birth to Jesus her son is there to see him die. The three streams of Christianity, the Roman Catholic Church of the West, the Orthodox Catholic Church of the East, and Protestantism, have historically viewed Mary somewhat differently. The Roman Church and the Orthodox Church call Mary the 'mother of God' (theotokos). This title developed very soon in the Early Church. Some have elevated Mary beyond what many consider biblical appropriateness. Some have not elevated Mary and given her the status she deserves. A center point for most Christians is to acknowledge and give Mary the honor she deserves as the mother of Jesus. Clearly she does not have the status of the Trinity nor is she to be worshiped. The Trinity alone is to be worshiped. However, she is to be venerated which means given the honor and adoration to which she is entitled for fulfilling the mission that God gave to her and her obedience to that role. Whatever one may believe about Mary, she certainly was the faithful and perfect mother and disciple.

Remember: Mary was faithful, loving, and obedient to God's calling and deserves to be properly venerated. Jesus wants no less.

66. Mature: *See Holiness and Perfection*

The word *mature* is translated in three places: 1 Corinthians 2:6; 14:20; and Philippians 3:15. The Greek word is *teleios* and in many translations, such as the *Revised Standard Version*, is translated "perfect." This use of the word does not mean absolute perfection as someone without fault or blemish. As with the words *holiness*, *perfection*, and *righteousness*, it is a matter of the "perfect living in the imperfect." If our hearts and lives are devoted to loving God and neighbor, being made in the image of Christ, and walking as He walked, we are declared *perfect* even though we make imperfect judgments in these clay jars in which we live.

Remember: We are meant to grow in grace and knowledge. Maturity means understanding what we believe and why. Maturity means knowing how to faithfully communicate our message better. Maturity means being careful about what we say and do. Maturity means confidently introducing people to Jesus. Maturity means shepherding others into the grace of holiness.

67. Means of Grace: *See Grace*

The means of grace, both those instituted by Jesus and those practical aspects of living in the faith, are vehicles by which we can personally encounter God. In the Wesleyan/Methodist heritage, the means of grace are described as the instituted means of grace—instituted by Jesus and the Holy Scriptures—and the prudential means of grace—practical means based on Early Church practices. Both are employed, according to Reverend Wesley, to ensure our salvation and our good works. The instituted means of grace through which we can encounter God are the Church (with emphasis on worship, both public and private), Scripture, prayer, the Sacraments (Holy Communion and Baptism), and fasting. Some of the practical means of grace that help us encounter God are reading Christian literature, study, daily devotional time with prayer and Scripture, Christian fellowship, and—for the first 200 years with Methodism but now almost entirely gone—the Wesleyan Class-Meetings. For Wesley these are the practical/prudential means of grace: Societies, Class-Meetings, and Bands (three ways of deepening one's Christian life) plus the Love Feasts (monthly informal, elongated singing, testimonies, Scripture reading, and Holy Communion), and the Covenant Service (a yearly renewal of vows and commitment on New Year's Eve). Many of these means of grace mentioned overlap all three streams of Christianity. The Roman Catholic Church and the Orthodox Catholic Church emphasize these means of grace in different forms.

Remember: We need the "means of grace" to help us grow as Christians, to strengthen and protect us against worldly lures, to keep us in the faith, and for fellowship.

68. Miracles: *"There are diversities of gifts, but the same Spirit . . . to another the working of miracles."* (1Corinthians 12:4, 10). *"Therefore we must give the more earnest heed to the things we have heard, lest we drift away, how shall we escape if we neglect so great a salvation, which at the first began to be spoken by the Lord, and was confirmed to us by those who heard Him. God also bearing witness both with signs and wonders, with various miracles, and gifts of the Holy Spirit, according to His own will?"* (Hebrews 2:1-6).

A miracle is the intervention of God in history. The intervention may occur around the use of natural order or it can be a supernatural event outside the known understanding of nature. The Creation event was a supernatural action of God. The Old Testament is replete with supernatural events caused by the intervention of God. The parting of the Red Sea would be one example. In the New Testament, the Incarnation is perhaps the first momentous miracle (John: 1:1-18). The virginal conception of Jesus, the God-man is another (Matthew 1-2). Jesus performed a multitude of miracles for several different reasons. Many times it was out of compassion for a person (Matthew 9:18, Matthew 9:33, John 4:48). Perhaps the greatest reason for His miracles was to proclaim the presence of the Kingdom of God and Himself as the inauguration of it (Matthew 12:28, 11:4-5, Mark 2:9-10). The Transfiguration with Moses and Elijah certainly revealed His position and power (Mark 9:1). Then again the Resurrection of Jesus was perhaps the greatest miracle of all and certainly without which there would be no Christianity. There are some who would say that the supernatural events which occurred in the Bible and Early Church times ceased after that period of Christian history. However, the overwhelming predominant belief in Christendom has always been and still is that the God Who has always been active in history through the Holy Spirit will continue to be active today and tomorrow. God's activity can be through what would be called natural events or it can be supernatural events. What we do not always know is why?

Remember: Birth is a miracle. Life is a miracle. Our resurrection will be a miracle. I am afraid supernatural actions are occurring all the time and we miss seeing them.

69. Mission: *"Jesus said, 'As the Father has sent me, I am sending you.'"* (John 20:21). *He also said, "Go, and make disciples."* (Matthew 28:19). *"The twelve Jesus sent out and commanded them, saying: 'Do not go into the way of the Gentiles, and do not enter a city of the Samaritans. But go rather to the lost sheep of the house of Israel. And as* *you go, preach, saying, the kingdom of heaven is at hand.'"* (Matthew 10:5-7).

Go and Send are non-negotiable ministries of the Christian Church. The going and sending can take many different forms. Not everyone in a congregation has to go and not everyone is sent. If a congregation does not have an intense passion for these ministries something is terribly wrong in that congregation or denomination. In Methodism, as one example, it used to be that a congregation spent 50 percent of its income on itself and 50 percent on mission/evangelism/outreach. A major emphasis at the Wednesday evening prayer meeting used to be on "going and sending." The "going and sending" can take many forms. It can be prayer, sending people, sending Bibles, sending money, visitation of visitors, shut-ins, and different works of compassion and justice. The list of mission work can be very long. Kingdom People hunger and thirst to introduce people to Jesus and rescue them from sin and bondage, to be healed spiritually, emotionally, perhaps physically and certainly eternally. The motivation is gratitude and love for what has been done for us. We joyfully cry out, "And can it be He died for me!"

Remember: A great salvation brings a great gratitude, a great gratitude will bring a great desire to serve.

70. Mystery: *"Let a man so consider us, as servants of Christ and stewards of the mysteries of God."* (1 Corinthians 4:1). *" . . .the mystery which has been hidden from ages and from generations, but now has been* *revealed to His saints. To them God willed to make known what are the riches of the glory of the mystery among the Gentiles: which is Christ in you, the hope of glory. Him we preach, warning every man in all wisdom, that we may present every man perfect in Christ Jesus."* (Colossians 1:26-28). *"Behold, I tell you a mystery: We shall not all sleep, but we shall all be changed—in a moment, in a twinkling of an eye, at the last trumpet. For the trumpet will sound, and the dead will be raised incorruptible, and we shall be changed. For this corruptible must put on incorruption, and this mortal put on immortality."* (1 Corinthians 15:51-53).

Remember: The mystery of the reality of the Kingdom of God can be known only through faith.

[N] **71. New Birth**: *"Jesus answered and said to him, 'Most assuredly, I say to you, unless one is born again, he cannot see the kingdom of God.'"* (John 3:3). *"Do not marvel that I said to you, you must be born again."* (John 3:7). *"...having been born again, not of corruptible seed but incorruptible, through the Word of God which lives and abides forever."* (1 Peter 1:23). *"Beloved, let us love one another, for love is of God; and everyone who loves is born of God and knows God."* (1 John 4:7).

Jesus stated the new birth was an imperative to the Christian life. John Wesley said, *"By reason we learn is that the new birth, without which we cannot enter into the kingdom of heaven, and what that holiness is, without which no man shall see the Lord."* Wesley believed that the new birth was necessary for salvation. For Wesley the new birth brought freedom from sin and by the power of the Holy Spirit; the promise of deliverance from sin and death. The new birth is marked by faith, hope, and love: faith, as a personal trust and assurance that Jesus Christ died for my sins; hope, as the inner witness that I have become a child of God; and love, that is poured into my heart by the Holy Spirit when I have justifying faith. For Wesley, until we have this new birth we are still in the clutches of Satan. New birth is not the same as baptism, justification, or sanctification, although it is the beginning of sanctification. It is when our selfish desires and ambitions are being replaced by the mind of Jesus Christ and we aspire only to love and serve in His Kingdom. Because holiness is the desire of God, the new birth is intended to move us into holiness.

Remember: A new birth can occur dramatically or it can occur quietly. The question is, "Has the love of Jesus come alive in my heart?"

[O] **72. Obedience:** *"For as by one man's disobedience many were made sinners, so by one Man's obedience many will be made righteous."* (Romans 15:19). *"For though we walk in the flesh, we do not war according to the flesh. For the weapons of our warfare are not carnal but mighty in God for pulling down strongholds, casting down arguments and every high thing that exalts itself against the knowledge of God, bringing every thought into captivity to the obedience to Christ."* (2 Corinthians 10:3-5).

The only perfectly obedient person in history was Jesus. Mary was significantly close. Jesus' obedience is mentioned specifically three times but alluded to multiple times: *"And being found in appearance as a man, He humbled Himself and became obedient to the point of death, even death of the cross."* (Philippians 2:8). *" . . .though He was a Son, yet He learned obedience by the things which He suffered."* (Hebrews 5:8). In the Old Testament there is a direct connection between hearing and obeying. *They were synonymous actions.* To hear the voice of God requires us to obey. Abraham was blessed because he heard and obeyed God's voice (Genesis 22:18). Jesus stands within the Old Testament understanding. Jesus says, *"Blessed are those who hear the word of God and obey it."* (Luke 11:28). Jesus is also clear that loving God and Jesus and being "friends" of Jesus are dependent upon obedience (John 14:18-15:17). Just as Jesus was obedient, followers are to be obedient to Him which then produces the blessing of salvation. *"And having been perfected, He became the author of eternal salvation to all who obey Him."* (Hebrews 5:9). Additionally, the Holy Spirit is given to those who obey. *"And we are His witnesses to these things, and so also is the Holy Spirit whom God has given to those who obey Him."* (Acts 5:32).

Remember: Love generates obedience and obedience has its own reward.

73. Original Sin: *See Sin-Original*

[P] **74. Paraclete:** *"But now I am going away to Him who sent Me, and none of you asks Me, 'Where are you going?' But because I have said these things to you, sorrow has filled your heart. Nevertheless I tell you the truth. It is to your advantage I go away; for if I do not go away, the Helper* *will not come to you; but if I depart, I will send Him to you. And when He comes He will convict the world of sin, and of righteousness and of judgment."* (John 16:5-9).

The word paraclete comes from the Greek word *parakletos*. Throughout John 14, 15, and 16, Jesus makes the promise to His disciples that He will send the "helper", the "counselor." The concept of the Holy Paraclete is one who helps, teaches, strengthens, advises, encourages, leads, and advocates. Of course, Jesus is talking about the Holy Spirit.

Remember: We have a Holy Paraclete working for us today.

75. Pastor: *"And He Himself gave some to be apostles, some prophets, some evangelists, and some pastors and teachers."* (Ephesians 4:11). *"But when He* (Jesus) *saw the multitudes, He was moved to compassion for them, because they were weary and scattered, like sheep having no shepherd* (pastor)*."* (Matthew 9:36). *"The thief does not come except to steal, and to kill, and to destroy. I come that you may have life, and that you may have it more abundantly. I am the good shepherd. The good shepherd gives His life for the sheep."* (John 10:10-11). The Reverend John Wesley said he thought the maximum number of people he could pastor was thirty. The number thirty still holds true today. Any more than the number thirty becomes poor pastoring and certainly not the kind of pastoring Jesus envisioned. That concept is why in the Early Church each church had a number of elders (shepherds) and sometimes several bishops. Note that there were no mega-churches back then. Poor shepherding is a major reason for the disproportionate small number of worshipers in a congregation as compared to membership roles. *See Elder/Deacon/Bishop.*

Remember: The biblical concept and demand is that each sheep (person) needs a shepherd; one shepherd for thirty sheep.

76. Perfection: *"Then He opened His mouth and taught them, saying, 'Therefore you shall be perfect, just as your Father in heaven is perfect.'"* (Matthew 5:48). *"Him we preach, warning every man and teaching every man in all wisdom, that we may present every man perfect in Christ Jesus."* (Colossians 1:29). *"No one has seen God at any time. If we love one another, God abides in us, and His love has been perfected in us."* (1 John 4:12). *See Holiness, Sanctification, Mature.*

77. Persecution: *"And He opened His mouth and taught them, saying, 'Blessed are you when they revile and persecute you, and say all kinds of evil against you falsely for My sake. Rejoice and be exceedingly glad, for great is your reward in heaven, for so they persecuted the prophets who were before you.'"* (Matthew 5:2, 11-12). *"Yes, and all who desire to live godly in Christ Jesus will suffer persecution."* (2 Timothy 3:12).

In John, Jesus warns His disciples that *"the world"* will hate them, persecute them, and even kill them thinking they are serving God (John 14:18-16:4). The ethics, morals, and spiritual life of the Kingdom of God is not just radically different than the Kingdom of the world; they are diametrically opposed to each other. The life of love of God and neighbor, of compassionate sharing, giving, forgiveness, and healing severely challenges the life of arrogance and self-centeredness. There is no compromise between the two Kingdoms. By its very nature light challenges darkness and forces decisions. It is absolutely true that life in the Kingdom brings a peace, joy, contentment, and happiness that is found nowhere else. It does not mean we will be excluded from conflict with the world. In reality, many times it is the opposite. The presumably Christian preaching and teaching that in one form or another tells us we will be "healthy, wealthy, and wise" is a false and dangerous message. Unfortunately, that teaching does appeal to our baser desires and therefore can be very appealing. In the real world, persecution for being a Christian may or may not come but conflict definitely will for real Christians.

Remember: Following Jesus may bring persecution but following Jesus will also bring peace, joy, and eternal life.

78. Perseverance (Jesus said) *"But he who endures to the end will be saved."* (Matthew 10:22). *"For you have need of endurance so that after you have done the will of God, you may receive the promise."* (Hebrews 10:36). *"If we endure we shall also reign with Him."* (2 Timothy 2:12).

In Hebrews 10:36, Jesus has given us the promise that he will preserve us to the uttermost. In John 6:37-40, Jesus is saying that He will in no way cast out anyone who comes to Him in faith. Jesus will on our last day lift us up to Him. Ephesians 6:18 advises us to be watchful with prayer and supplication in the Spirit so that we might persevere to the end (2 Peter 1:6; Revelation 2:3; 3:10). It is called "final perseverance."

Remember: We are able to persevere to the end and be saved because God's grace has given us the Holy Spirit who empowers us to persevere. We only need the desire and supplication.

79. Pharisee: The word Pharisee is found continually throughout the New Testament. Most scholars agree that the movement began in the Second Century, B.C., and ended after the fall of Jerusalem in A.D. 70. The emphasis of the Pharisaic movement however did become a highly influential group in the future rabbinic Judaism. Importantly, it was a lay movement as opposed to the Sadducees which was a priestly group. The Pharisees were an extremely devout group that adhered to the Mosaic laws and regulations. As opposed to the Sadducees they believed in three important differences. The Pharisees believed in angels and spirits, in the resurrection of the dead, and in the coming of the Messiah. It is difficult sometimes to have an accurate perspective on the Pharisees. Mostly, we have a very negative and pejorative picture of them. However, The Pharisees warn Jesus of a plot against Him (Luke 13:31). In spite of their rigid dietary regulations, they invite Him to partake of meals with them (Luke 7:36-50; 14:1). Most Pharisees finally could not accept Jesus as the Messiah. However, it was the Pharisees who helped Jesus' followers to survive (Acts 5:34; 23:6-9). Many

Pharisees, like many priests, did come to believe in Jesus (John 3:17, 45-53; 9:13-38).

Remember: It is easy and wrong to judge a whole group of people by some of the group. Without doubt the Pharisaic movement desired and did become an intensely dedicated group to that which they understood as righteousness. Jesus condemned them because of their arrogant self-righteousness and refusal to accept Him. Some Pharisees denied Jesus and some became devoted faithful Christians.

80. Prayer: Prayer is essentially communication with another person. In the Christian context it involves a deep binding living relationship with each person of the Trinity. The communication can take a multitude of forms: listening, praise, thanksgiving, confession, petition, intercession, supplication,and silence. Prayer may take words and it may not take any. However, the Bible would seem to indicate that the prayer of the heart, or in the Spirit, is the highest form of prayer. (Matthew 6:5-13; 21:22; Romans 8:26; Philippians 4:6; 1 Thessalonians 5:17). God always looks to the intention of the heart and the Spirit helps us to pray.

Remember: Prayer is not bound by forms although there are many forms that help with praying. For example, reading can be a form of prayer.

81. Presbyter: *See Elders*

82. Prevenient Grace: *See Grace*

Prevenient grace is that grace that precedes other grace. It precedes all human decision and endeavor. Grace always means that it is God who takes the initiative and implies the priority of God's action on needy sinners. The whole point of grace is the understanding that it does not start with us, it starts with God. It is not earned or merited by us but is freely given to us while we were yet sinners (Romans 5:8, 10; 2 Corinthians 8:9, 1 John 4:10, 19). Prevenient grace is God reaching out to us before we even know it.

Remember: It is first of all God in His immeasurable love reaching out to us to bring us to repentance, to justification, to sanctification, to holiness in Christ Jesus to eternal life.

83. Prophets: *"Now there was one, Anna, a prophetess, the daughter of Phanuel, of the tribe of Asher."* (Luke 2:36). *"Then Jesus spoke to the multitudes and to His disciples, saying, 'Therefore, indeed, I send you prophets, wise men, and scribes.'"* (Matthew 23:1, 34). *"But to each of us grace was given according to the measure of Christ's gift. And He Himself gave some to be apostles, some prophets, some evangelists, some pastors and teachers, for the equipping of the saints for the work of ministry, for the edifying of the body of Christ."* (Ephesians 4:7, 11-12).

In the Old Testament the prophet is one who witnesses, testifies, or speaks on behalf of God. The prophet is the one who has been given the gift of hearing God's voice and knowing what needs to be said to the people at a specific time or event in history. The message may be one of calling them back to repentance and faithfulness or it may be warning the people of an impending disaster or threat. Or also in the Old Testament it was the prophecies of the coming of the Messiah—Jesus. It is God who calls and inspires the prophet (Jeremiah 20:7). In the Old Testament there are four of what are called Major Prophets: Isaiah, Jeremiah, Ezekiel, and Daniel. There are twelve Minor Prophets: Hosea, Joel, Amos, Obadiah, Jonah, Micah, Nahum, Habakkuk, Zephaniah, Haggai, Zechariah, and Malachi. There were also other prophets. After several centuries of prophetic silence, John the Baptist is seen as the last of the Old Testament prophets. In the New Testament, a prophetic ministry is exercised by both men and women (Acts 2:28; 21:10; 15:32; 21:8-10). In the Early Church, prophets were important to the life of the community fulfilling numerous roles. They were second in importance to the Apostles (1 Corinthians 12:28-31, Ephesians 2:20; 4:11). As were the Old Testament prophets, the New Testament prophets were under the guidance of the Holy Spirit (Acts 11:27-28; 21:11). Throughout Church history the Spirit has raised up prophets. It is helpful to think about prophecy as having two dimensions. One is foretelling and one is forthtelling . When Isaiah and other Old Testament prophets prophesied about the coming of certain events in history or the coming of the Messiah and what would happen to Him, it is called foretelling. The second form of prophecy is forthtelling. It involves the kind of insight and discernment to understand that if a person, a people, or the Church thinks and behaves in a certain manner that is contrary to the Word of God there will be consequences for those actions. The consequences are almost always dramatic. Prophets who confront a person, a people, a church, a nation with reality have never been popular.

Remember: Today the Spirit of Christ is raising up men and women to speak to us, the nation, to the Church. It may be warnings, or blessings, or predictions of the future. But they are speaking the Word of God.

84. Providence: *"And we know that all things work together for good to those who love God, to those who are called according to His purpose."* (Romans 8:28). *"Then they came to a place called Gethsemane; and He said to His disciples, 'Sit here while I pray.' And He took Peter, James, and John with Him, and He began to be troubled and deeply distressed. Then He said to them, 'My soul is exceedingly sorrowful, even to death. Stay here and watch." He went a little farther, and fell on the ground, and prayed that if it were possible, the hour might pass from Him. And he said, 'Abba, Father, all things are possible for You. Take this cup from Me; nevertheless, not My will, but what You will.'"* (Mark 14:33-36).

The word comes from the Latin and means "to provide or to make preparation for". God's will, His activity, is so pervasive in Judaic/Christian history that it is difficult to describe the meaning of the word, except we know it when we see it. Put simply, it is God's sovereign care in directing, providing for, and governing His creation, especially His care for the faithful. When we say, "That was providential," we are saying that it was God's will and intention. His presence.

Remember: God's will, His activity, His direction, in another word, His providence, is always with us and around us.

[R] **85. Reconciliation**: *"For if when we were enemies we were reconciled to God through the death of His Son, much more, having been reconciled, we shall be saved by His life. And not only that, but we also rejoice in God through our Lord Jesus Christ, through whom we have now received the reconciliation."* (Romans 5:10). *"Now all things are of God, who has reconciled us to Himself through Jesus Christ, and has given us the ministry of reconciliation, that is, that God was in Christ reconciling the world to Himself, not imputing their trespasses to them, and has committed to us the word of reconciliation."* (2 Corinthians 5:18-19).

Reconciliation basically means to "restore" or "reunite." The word used in Scripture for *reconciliation* implies transformation. It is the transformation or change from enmity with God to friendship with God. It is not God who is reconciled, but we who are reconciled to God. The enmity and divisiveness was on our part. It is God's grace and mercy that makes this possible through Jesus Christ. Paul in second Corinthians 5:18–19 says it beautifully. *"Now all things are of God, who has reconciled us to Himself through Jesus Christ, and has given us the ministry of reconciliation, that is, that God was in Christ reconciling the world to Himself, not imputing* [attributing or charging] *their trespasses to them, and has committed to us the word of reconciliation."* The removal of hostility and the barriers between mankind and God allows for those same hostilities and barriers to be removed between people. In fact, it is our task to assist in bringing about that reconciliation between people.

Remember: Forgiveness and reconciliation is what God did for us and what we are required, to the best of what is possible, to do with others.

86. Regeneration: *"But when the kindness and the love of God our Savior toward man appeared, not by works of righteousness which we have done, but according to His mercy He saved us, through the washing of regeneration and renewing of the Holy Spirit."* (Titus 3:5-6). Jesus said, *"Most assuredly. I say to you, unless one is born again, he cannot see the kingdom of God."* (John 3:2).

Regeneration is that work of the Spirit in us whereby we begin the change from an arrogant self-centered person to becoming one of God's people seeking God's holy ways. It is the heart's desire for a new life (Romans 3:9-18; 8:7). The whole concept of a new birth is meant to emphasize the radical new change beginning in a person. It is caused by the supernatural power of God. It is a new starting point in a person's life, not an end in itself. It is part of justification (pardon) but is not justification itself. It is a part of being born again but it is what happens after the new birth as the Holy Spirit begins a work within us.

Remember: The Spirit seeks the changed heart by which He begins the generation of the changed person.

87. Repentance: *"Now after John was put in prison, Jesus came to Galilee, preaching the gospel of the kingdom of God, and saying, 'The Time is fulfilled, and the kingdom of God is at hand. Repent and believe in the gospel.'"* (Mark 1:14). *"Truly, these times of ignorance God overlooked, but now commands all men everywhere to repent, because He has appointed a day on which He will judge the world in righteousness by the Man whom He has ordained. He has given assurance of this to all by raising Him from the dead."* (Acts 17:30-31). *"So they* (disciples) *went out and preached that people should repent."* (Mark 6:12). *"Then Peter said to them, 'Repent, and let every one of you be baptized in the name of Jesus Christ for the remission of sins; and you shall receive the gift of the Holy Spirit.'"* (Acts 2:38).

Literally, this word means "a change of heart and mind that produces a change in behavior." The question becomes, "What causes a person to radically change heart, mind, and behavior?" The Bible is abundantly clear it requires some degree of regret and or remorse for present or past actions. Except for Luke 17:3–4, it involves repentance from sin that leads to behavior change. The word is found extensively in the Bible: nine times in the Synoptic Gospels (Matthew, Mark, and Luke), five times in Acts, twelve times in Revelation, and eight times in the messages to the churches. Unfortunately, for many of us it is a lifetime activity. *See sin/original.*

Remember: Jesus' message of repentance was directed at God believers who thought they had all the right theology and right behavior but it is meant for all people. Repentance is the result of genuine remorse but repentance overcomes remorse, shame, and guilt.

88. Resurrection of Jesus: *"Blessed be the God and Father of our Lord Jesus Christ, who according to His abundant mercy has begotten us again to a living hope through the resurrection of Jesus Christ from the dead, to an inheritance incorruptible and undefiled and that does not fade away, reserved in heaven for you, who are kept by the power of God through faith for salvation ready to be revealed in the last time."* (1 Peter 1:3–5). *"Therefore, of these men who have accompanied us all the time that the Lord went in and out among us, beginning from the baptism of John to that day when He was taken up from us, one of these must become a witness with us to His resurrection. And they proposed two: Joseph called Barsabas, who was surnamed Justus, and Matthias."* (Acts 1:21-23). *"And with great power the apostles gave witness to the resurrection of the Lord Jesus. And great grace was upon them all."* (Acts 4:33).

The resurrection event proclaims the mighty, loving act of God for humanity and God's desire that we should all love and live with Him forever. For Christians, it is the most glorious event. The people who witnessed the life, death, and resurrection of Jesus, as well as the people who were with Him after the resurrection, were totally convinced that Jesus had indeed been raised from the dead in bodily form. The resurrection of Jesus is chronicled in every book of the New Testament with clear and convincing proclamation (1 Corinthians 15:3; Romans 1:1–4; Romans 8:11; Philippians 2:9–11; Philippians 3:10). In a dramatic moment in history, God proclaimed through the resurrection of Jesus that He had broken Satan's power of sin and death over humanity. We are now free to choose a new life in which sin and death have been conquered. Additionally, Scripture gives us the promise of our own resurrection (Romans 6:1–11; John 11:17–27; 14:18–21; 1 John 5:11; and in multiple other places in the New Testament).

Remember: The physical Resurrection of Jesus broke the power of sin and death and insured our resurrection.

89. Righteousness: *"Blessed are those who hunger and thirst for righteousness."* (Matthew 5:6). *" . . .who Himself bore our sins in His own body on the tree, that we, having died to sins, might live to righteousness—by whose stripes you were healed."* (1 Peter 2:24). *"And now, little children, abide in Him, that when He appears, we may have confidence and not be ashamed before Him at His coming. If you know that He is righteous, you know that everyone who practices righteousness is born of Him."* (1 John 2:28-29).

There are over 100 mentions of righteousness in the New Testament alone. The Reverend John Wesley makes a sharp contrast between "the righteousness which is of the law" and "the righteousness which is of faith" (See his sermon "The Righteousness of Faith"). The righteousness of faith understands all people to be sinners before God and that it is God's work through Jesus Christ that gives us salvation and thereby makes us righteous. Wesley thus understood that being righteous in God's presence could not be earned. However, Wesley strongly believed that righteous acts would flow out of our lives because of our new relationship with God, which produced gratitude and obedience to "the righteousness of the law." Being righteous therefore means being just (concerned with justice); being obedient to the will of God; being blameless, pure, and undefiled; having perfect love; being sanctified; and being holy as God is holy. Acts of righteousness do not earn salvation but are the natural outcome of salvation.

Remember: Righteousness is the fruit of salvation and the active indwelling of the Holy Spirit with whom we respond in faith, love, and gratitude for God's great gift to us.

[S] **90. Sacrament**: A sacrament is a rite in which God's presence and grace are believed to be uniquely active. The word is derived from the Latin word *sacramentum,* which means to take an oath of allegiance or an obligation. Based on the writing of Saint Augustine (354–430), the Anglican Catechism and the Methodist Catechism both defined a sacrament as *"an outward and visible sign of an inward and spiritual grace given unto us (ordained by Christ Himself) as a means whereby we receive this grace, and a pledge to assure us thereof."* Thus the Sacraments are means of grace. In Protestantism, there are only two Sacraments—the Holy Eucharist (Holy Communion) and Baptism. These two Sacraments are recognized by all Christian churches, though the Baptists use the word *ordinance* instead of *sacrament* and usually call communion, the Lord's Supper. The Roman Catholic Church of the West recognizes seven Sacraments—the Holy Eucharist, Baptism, Penance, Holy Matrimony, Holy orders, Confirmation, and Extreme Unction (last rites) which is now practiced primarily as the anointing of the sick. The Orthodox Catholic Church of the East recognizes seven Sacraments but they are emphasized differently from the Roman Church. Baptism, Chrismation, the Eucharist, Repentance or Confession, Holy Orders, Holy Matrimony, and the Anointing of the Sick. While Protestants may recognize only two as Sacraments of Christ, I think we would all agree the ones affirmed as sacraments by the Roman Catholic Church and the Orthodox Catholic Church are central elements of Christianity. *See Eucharist and Baptism.*

Remember: Sacraments are "means of grace" which are experiential ways meant for us to receive the benefits of God's Grace and Presence. Although the three streams of Christianity place different embassies and understandings on what is a Sacrament all would agree on the reality of the grace of God in all seven of the activities of the Holy Spirit and the undeserved wonderful effect on our lives. Extremely important is that all three streams of Christianity agree on a centrally important activity of Communion which is the "real presence" of Christ in Holy Communion.

91. Sacrifice of Christ (Atonement): *"For indeed Christ our Passover was sacrificed for us."* (1 Corinthians 5:7). *"And as they were eating, Jesus took bread, blessed and* *broke it, and gave it to the disciples, and said, 'Take, eat, this is my body.' Then He took the cup, and gave thanks, gave it to them, saying, 'Drink from it, all of you. For this my blood of the new covenant, which is shed for many for the remission of sins.'"* (Matthew 26:26-28). *"For even the Son of Man did not come to be served, but to serve, and to give His life a ransom for many."* (Mark 10:45).

The word *atonement* (at-one-ment) incorporates the idea of reconciliation. The classical theory was the view of the Early Church, of Paul, Irenaeus (c.115–c. 200), Origen (c. 185–c. 254), Athanasius (c. 295–373), Augustine (354–430), Martin Luther (1483–1546), John Wesley (1703–1791), and has been the overwhelmingly prevalent view of the body of Christendom throughout the centuries. The primary understanding is that we humans are under the power of sin and death. It is Satan who holds this power. It is the Incarnation, God coming in Jesus, who defeats this power and sets us free. It is God who performs this act, not humans. It is the sacrifice of Jesus (God) who accomplishes this victory over sin and death, reconciles us with God, and provides the way to eternal life. Now this sacrifice was given and accomplished on the Cross of Christ.

Remember: We know the atonement to be real when in our hearts we recognize our freedom from and power over sin and death and can say, "Christ died on the cross for me."

92. Sadducees: The Sadducees were a very powerful group from about the Second Century, B.C., until the late First Century, A.D. Most scholars agree they were a priestly order which also included wealthy men. Unlike the Pharisees, the Sadducees did not believe in angels and supernatural beings, nor the coming of the Messiah, nor the resurrection of the dead with heaven or hell, so consequently they did not believe in "repentance" as necessary. Of course, repentance was the first central admonition of both John the Baptist and Jesus. It was a message that John the Baptist and Jesus both preached and taught. Clearly the Sadducees were a very secular kind of group. It is easy to see why they were so severely opposed to Jesus. The Sadducees opposed Jesus on theological grounds. But probably more importantly Jesus was a direct threat to the status quo.

Remember: The Bible warns us that in every age there will be people, even religious leaders, opposed to Jesus. Additionally, every age has counterfeit Christians who basically believe what the Sadducees believed.

93. Saints: *"To the church of God which is at Corinth, to those who are sanctified in Christ Jesus, called to be saints, with all who in every place call on the name of Jesus Christ our Lord, both theirs and ours."* (1 Corinthians 1:2). *"Now it came to pass Peter went through all parts of the country that he also came down to the saints who dwelt in Lydda."* (Acts 9:32). *"Now may our God and Father Himself, and our Lord Jesus Christ, direct our way to you. And may the Lord make you increase and abound in love to one another and to all, just as we do to you, so that He may establish your hearts blameless in holiness before our*

God and Father at the coming of our Lord Jesus Christ with all the saints." (1 Thessalonians 3:11-13).

In the New Testament the word "saint" is applied to all believers in Christ Jesus. It is used to identify a brother or sister in the faith (Colossians 1:2). The saints are the people of the Way, the Church (1 Corinthians 1:2). The Book of Ephesians has a strong emphasis on the unity of the Church and refers to "all the saints" (Ephesians 1:15; 3:8, 18; 6:18). As time passed the word began to be more exclusively applied to those who had been extraordinarily faithful, usually in martyrdom. All the major Christian denominations hold in special honor such persons and this is why so many churches are named St. Matthew, St. Mark, St. Luke, St. John, etc.

Remember: We are all meant to be saints. We would do well to remember and learn from all those "extraordinary" saints of history, many of whom died and are today dying for Jesus.

94. Salvation: *"Nor is there salvation in any other, for there is no other name under heaven given among men by which we must be saved."* (Acts 4:12). *"For I am not ashamed of the gospel of Christ, for it is the power of God to salvation for everyone who believes, for the Jew first and also for the Greeks."* (Romans 1:16). *"Now I rejoice, not that you were made sorry, but that your sorrow led to repentance. For you were made sorry in a godly manner, that you might suffer loss from us in nothing. For godly sorrow produces repentance leading to salvation, not to be regretted; but the sorrow of the world produces death."*

(2 Corinthians 7:9-10). *"In Him you also trusted, after you heard the word of truth, the gospel of your salvation; in whom also, having believed you were sealed with the Holy Spirit of promise."* (Ephesians 2:13). *"In this you greatly rejoice, though now for a little while, if need be, you have been grieved by various trials, that the genuineness of your faith, being much more precious than gold that perishes, though it is tested by fire, may be found to praise, honor, and glory at the revelation of Jesus Christ, — receiving the end of your faith, the salvation of your souls."* (1 Peter 1:6-7, 9).

It is important to keep the end in mind. The end of all things will occur when God has completely destroyed the work of Satan, and the reign of God, the Kingdom of God, is the only Kingdom. The core message of salvation is that by the grace of God (Ephesians 2:8) we receive faith (prevenient grace) to believe the Gospel of Jesus Christ. The Gospel is the saving power of God at work in the world and is available to all who would receive Christ in their hearts, become like Him in His death, and walk as He walked. (See particularly Philippians 3:9–10, Romans 4:16; 10:9; and 1 Peter 1:5). In the New Testament, there are over 160 references to the words *save* and *salvation*. Salvation is simultaneously already accomplished, happening in the present, and will be a future reality. Example of salvation accomplished: In the Synoptic Gospels, we hear, *"And Jesus said to him, 'Today salvation has come to this house, because he also is a son of Abraham; for the Son of Man has come to seek and save that which was lost.'"* (Luke 19:9–10). Being presently saved means that by the grace of God we have been rescued, our relationship has been restored, and we are secure against the Day of the Lord, that day when all will be judged (Romans 8:24; 2 Timothy 1:9; Titus 3:5). Example of future salvation: In Matthew 1:21, we hear that Jesus will save His people from their sins. Approximately 20 percent of the salvation references are about that final day when the Kingdom of God will be fully established (Romans 13:11; 1 Peter 1:5). Therefore we can say, "I have been saved; I am being saved; I will be saved." For a more complete understanding of the biblical concept of salvation, read the Reverend John Wesley's sermon "The Scripture Way of Salvation."

Remember: Being rescued and made secure from sin and death is a present event, (justification) being formed in the image of Christ is an ongoing event, (sanctification) heaven is a future eternal event (glorification). I have been saved, I am being saved, I will be saved.

95. Sanctification: Jesus said: *"And for their sakes I sanctify Myself, that they also may be sanctified by the truth."* (John 17:19). *"...that I might be a minister of Jesus Christ to the Gentiles, ministering the gospel of God, that the suffering of the Gentiles might be acceptable, sanctified by the Holy Spirit."* (Romans 15:16). *"Now may the God of peace Himself sanctify you completely; and may your whole spirit, soul, and body be preserved blameless at the coming of our Lord Jesus Christ. He who calls you is faithful and will do it."* (1 Thessalonians 5:23-24). *See Holiness and Mature..*

96. Satan: *"And He was there in the wilderness forty days, tempted by Satan, and was with the wild beasts; and the angels ministered to Him."* (Mark 1:13). Jesus said, *"So ought not this woman, being a daughter of Abraham, whom Satan has bound—think of it—for eighteen years, be loosed from this bond on the Sabbath?"* (Luke 13:16). *"...lest Satan should take advantage of us; for we are not ignorant of his devices."* (2 Corinthians 2:11). *"Therefore we wanted to come to you—even I, Paul, time and again—but Satan hindered us."* (1 Thessalonians 2:18). *"Be sober, be vigilant, because your adversary the devil walks about like a roaring lion, seeking whom he may devour."* (1 Peter 5:8). *See Evil One/Devil.*

97. Scripture (Holy Bible): *"For what does the Scripture say?"* (Romans 4:3). Jesus said, *"But all this was done that the Scriptures of the prophets might be fulfilled."* (Matthew 26:56). *"And beginning at Moses and all the Prophets, He expounded to them in all the Scriptures the things concerning Himself."* (Luke 24:27). *"All Scripture is given by inspiration from God, and is profitable for doctrine, for reproof, for correction, for instruction in righteousness."* (2 Timothy 3:16).

The word *Bible* comes from the Greek word *biblia,* meaning "books." The word *Scripture* means "sacred writings." When "the Scriptures" are mentioned in the New Testament, it refers to the Old Testament because the New Testament had obviously not been written. Now we use the word to refer to both the Old and New Testaments. Until the Twentieth Century, the Old and New Testaments were called the Old and New Covenants because they represented a covenant, an agreement, a contract between God and His people. Of course it was Jesus who initiated the New Covenant by His life, death, resurrection, and ascension. The Bible was written by many different people from about 900 B.C. to A.D. 100. The Council of Hippo in A.D. 393 confirmed a list of these writings, which were called a *canon* of inspired books. A canon refers to a standard measurement. Applied to the sacred writings, it refers to those writings that are authoritative for faith, life, and the Church. The Protestant Bible has thirty-nine books in the Old Covenant, the Orthodox and Roman Bible has forty-six books. These cover the Law (five books), the Prophets (twenty-one books), the Writings (thirteen books), and then the Second Canon (seven books called the *apocrypha*), which the Protestant Bible usually does not include. *Apocrypha* means "hidden" or "secret." Applied to the Scriptures, it refers to the time "in between the testaments" and does not have the same authority as the Old or New Testament. The New Testament is made up of twenty-seven books: the Gospels (four books), the Acts of the Apostles (one book), the Letters of Paul (thirteen), Other Letters (eight), and the Revelation of John (one). *See Scripture (Truth and Authority of) and Word of God.*

98. Scripture (Truth and Authority of): God has made Himself known, at least as much as He deemed necessary, in the "writings" called Scripture. God's revelation concerning His nature and will is made known to us in historical words and actions and recorded for us in Scripture, the Word of God. The authority to command us to understand

and obey God's Word comes from Jesus Himself. Jesus understood His Bible, what we now call the Old Covenant, more commonly called the Old Testament, to be commands that He was called to understand and obey. These are exemplified in Scriptures. (Matthew 4:4, 7, 10; 5:19–20; 19:4–6; 26:31, 52–54; Luke 4:16–21; 16:17; 18:31–33; 22:37; 24:25–27; Matthew 5:17–18; 26:24; John 5:46). The authors of the New Covenant, commonly called the New Testament, describe the biblical writings as God's Word, as Scripture with all the reverence and recognition of authority due it. All the books of the Bible, which include the thirty-nine written before Jesus and the twenty-seven written after Him, in all their different forms and expressions must, as Jesus commanded, be understood and obeyed as God's revelation to us about Himself, us, our relationship to Him, and our grateful obedience to His will. The essence is that Scripture was an authority to be understood and obeyed for Jesus and He commanded the same for us. *See Scripture (Holy Bible) and Word of God.*

Remember: The Bible/Scripture is the essential and reliable authority for faith and practice of the Christian life. All other writings of whatever nature, even those having some authority are simply commentaries on Scripture.

99. Second Coming: *"Then they will see the Son of Man coming in the clouds with great power and glory."* (Mark 13:26). *"You have heard Me say to you, I am going away and coming back to you."* (John 14:28). *"Now,* *brethren, concerning the coming of our Lord Jesus Christ and our gathering to Him, we ask you, not to be soon shaken in mind or troubled, either by spirit or by word or by letter, as if from us, as though the day of Christ had come."* (2 Thessalonians 2:1-2). *"Therefore be patient brethren, until the coming of the Lord."*(James 5:8). *"Behold, He is coming with clouds, and every eye will see Him, even they who pierced Him. —'I am the Alpha and the Omega, the Beginning and the End', says the Lord, 'who is and who was and who is to come, the Almighty.'"* (Revelation 1:7-8).

The Second Coming of Jesus to earth is mentioned multiple times in the New Testament. It will be both physical and personal. In His last important teaching in Matthew 24-25, Jesus speaks of his return in parables. Some of the passages mentioned are Matthew 24:44; 1 Corinthians 15:23; Philippians 3:20; Acts 1:11; Colossians 3:4; 2 Timothy 4:8; Hebrews 9:28; Mark 8:38; 2Thessalonians 1:10; John 5:28-29; Romans 8:17-18 and Revelations 1:7. The purpose of the Coming is to completely establish the Kingdom of God. It is the time in history when as the Bible says *"every knee shall bow, in heaven and on earth, and under the earth, and every tongue that Jesus Christ is Lord, to the glory of God the father."* (Philippians 2:10-11). No one knows the time of His Coming so we need to be prepared all the time.

Remember: Jesus our Christ who has ascended to our Father will return again someday to the earth and bring history to its final consummation. We need to be prepared every day for His coming.

100. Sin: *"...for all have sinned and fall short of the glory of God."* (Romans 3:23). *"If we say we have no sin, we deceive ourselves, and the truth is not in us."* (1 John 1:8). *"For the wages of sin is death, but the gift of God is eternal life in Christ Jesus our Lord."* (Romans 6:23). *"For if by one man's disobedience many were made sinners, so also by one Man's obedience many will be made righteous."* (Romans 5:19-20).

The doctrine or teaching on this subject begins with the teaching on Original Sin. Without a proper understanding of original sin we will never adequately comprehend the Christian message. The underlying premise of this teaching is that we come into this world seriously flawed (depraved). However we may choose to explain it, the reality is that we have this immense propensity for self-centeredness and self-gratification that denies a love for and obedience to God and His laws. The ensuing consequences result in broken relationships, suffering, and estrangement from God. It is noteworthy that Jesus never defined *sin*; He simply accepted the reality of our behavior and dealt with it. Both the Old Testament and the New Testament have several variations for the word or words that relate to sin. The direct translation into an English equivalent is extremely difficult. The New Testament has approximately seven or eight different ways to interpret the Greek word for sin, *hamartia*, and thus we miss the various understandings unless we have carefully studied all of them and their contexts. Many attempts have been made to separate out the levels of sin. The segmentation includes mortal and venial, voluntary and involuntary, omission and commission, inward and outward, etc. One thing we know is that we either have a heart for our own selfish desires or we have a heart for the things of God. One last note here is that the biblical proclamation is that *"Christ died for our sins."* (1 Corinthians 15:3; Romans 4:25; Galatians 1:4; 2 Corinthians 5:19). And one of our favorites, Romans 5:8, *"But God demonstrates His own love toward us, in that while we were still sinners, Christ died for us." See Sin, Original.*

Remember: Sin is real and so is ours. There is only one place of healing. The place is Jesus the Christ.

101. Sin, Original: *'Therefore, just as through one man sin entered the world, and death through sin, and thus death spread to all men, because all sinned—(for until the law sin was in the world, but sin is not imputed when there is no law) Nevertheless death reigned from Adam to Moses even over those who had not sinned according to the likeness of the transgression of Adam, who is a type of Him who was to come. But the free gift is not like the offense. For if by one man's offense many died, much more the grace of God and the gift by the grace of the one Man, Jesus Christ, abounded to many."* (Romans 5:12-15). *"Therefore the law is holy, and the commandment holy and just and good. Has then what is good become death to me? Certainly not! But sin, that it might appear sin, was producing death in me through what is good, so that sin through the commandment might become exceedingly sinful. For we know that the law is spiritual, but I am carnal, sold under sin. For what I am doing, I do not understand. For what I will to do, that I do not practice; but what I hate, that I do. If, then, I do what I will not to* *do, I agree with the law that it is good. But now, it is no longer I who do it, but sin that dwells in me. For I know that in me (that is, in my flesh) nothing good dwells; for to will is present with me, but how to perform what is good I do not find—O wretched man that I am! Who will deliver me from this body of death? I thank God—through Jesus Christ our Lord."* (Romans 7: 12-25).

The term "original sin" was coined by Bishop Irenaeus in the second century. The Christian understanding of life is that every human being comes into the world stained with what is called Original Sin. It is explained and understood as the consequence of the disobedient actions of Adam and Eve. It is humanity's propensity to self-centeredness and selfishness, and beyond that to horrific acts of extreme cruelty, brutality, and murder. That humanity from the beginning has committed these acts is unquestionable. The only question raised by philosophers and theologians and by any reflective person through history is "why?" The consequence of that stain is threefold: mortality, a tendency to sin and evil, and alienation from our Creator. As a side note, Original Sin does not carry guilt; guilt is only credited to us when we commit sinful or evil acts. Even though we are born with this depravity, we are free to choose how we act, and those decisions are what produce sins credited to our account. Regardless of what explanation we use to interpret this reality, the issue becomes, "How then do we overcome and control our corrupt nature?" The answer in its most simple and truest form is faith in the atoning sacrifice of Jesus Christ. *See Sin and Sacrifice.*

Remember: The words original sin or depravity may feel like an insult to our self-esteem, reason, or our "innate goodness". However, acceptance of it is the only reasonable answer to our human condition which is our human preponderance to commit or participate in sin and evil.

102. Spiritual Gifts: Spiritual gifts are mentioned primarily in four places in the Bible (Romans 12:1-8; 1 Corinthians 12:1-30; 1 Corinthians 14:1-40; Ephesians 4:7-16). One needs to look at all four to see the total number of spiritual gifts. There are a variety of spiritual gifts given as God's grace determines. Spiritual gifts are given in a measure as God determines. Spiritual gifts are to be used to build up the body of Christ, the Church. Spiritual gifts are meant to bring unity to the body of Christ. It is important to know what our spiritual gifts are so we can exercise them in the body for the glory of God, to build up the Church and for our own satisfaction at doing works that contribute to the whole.

Remember: We are to use whatever measure of spiritual gift given to the best of our ability never comparing ourselves to other believers or elevating ourselves above others.

103. Steward: *"And the Lord said, 'Who then is that faithful and wise steward, whom his master will make ruler over his household?'"*(Luke 12:42). *"Let a man so consider us, as servants of Christ and stewards of the mysteries of God."* (1Corinthians 4:1). *"As each one has received a gift, minister* *it to one another, as good stewards of the manifold grace of God."* (1 Peter 4:10). *"He also said to His disciples; 'There was a certain rich man who had a steward, and an accusation was brought against him that this man was wasting his goods. So he called him and said to him. 'What is this I hear about you? Give an accountant of your stewardship, for you can no longer be steward.'"* (Luke 16:1-2).

The word *steward* first denotes the manager of a household or property (Luke 12:42). In one of the Reverend John Wesley's finest and most classic sermons, "The Good Steward," he articulates the biblical principle that everything we have is a gift from God and is to be used to contribute to the Kingdom of God. All that is given to us, our minds, our hearts, our wills, the spiritual gifts, the natural talents, the material resources, the opportunities in life, are all entrusted to us as stewards or managers and are to be used for God's purposes. The New Testament talks about stewards being preachers and teachers of the Word of God and doctrine (1 Corinthians 4:1; 2:2; 2 Corinthians 9:6–8; 1 Peter 4:10); of Elders and Bishops in churches (Titus 1:7); and of believers generally (1 Peter 4:10). It was the Reverend Wesley's understanding that every thought and action was to be brought into submission and obedience to Jesus Christ, *"bringing every thought into captivity to the obedience of Christ."* (2 Corinthians 10:5).

Remember: We are either good or bad stewards. We will be held accountable for how we have used what God has given to us.

104. Tongues-Speaking In: *See Spiritual Gifts* The biblical word *glossolalia* literally means "speaking in tongues". Unfortunately and unnecessarily this spiritual gift has many times throughout Christian history been controversial and divisive with people having radically different opinions about this gift. Mention of this gift is found in 1 Corinthians 12 where spiritual gifts are mentioned. 1 Corinthians 14:1-40 mentions higher gifts. Paul warns about too much emphasis on this gift urging believers to concentrate on love. In 1 Corinthians 13:1, Paul also emphasized the need to communicate the gospel intelligibly, especially to non-believers (1 Corinthians 14:2). There have been some who think that this gift was only for the Early Church and it ceased therein. Others have raised this gift up to where one has not been baptized or received the Holy Spirit without this gift. Most Christians throughout Christian history affirm this gift as legitimate but believe it must be used wisely within the Christian community. *See Spiritual Gifts.* For a complete understanding read Francis MacNutt, *Pentecostalism.*

105. Transfiguration: *"Now after six days Jesus took Peter, James, and John his brother, led them up on a high mountain by themselves; and He was transfigured before them. His face shone like the sun, and His clothes became as white as light. And behold, Moses and Elijah appeared to them, talking with Him. Then Peter answered and said to Jesus, 'Lord it is good for us to be here; if you wish, let us make three tabernacles, one for you, one for Moses and one for Elijah.' While he was still speaking, behold, a bright cloud overshadowed them; and suddenly a voice came out of the cloud, saying, 'This is my beloved Son, in whom I am* *well pleased. Hear Him. 'And when the disciples heard it, they fell on their faces and were greatly afraid. But Jesus came and touched them and said, "Arise, and do not be afraid.' When they had lifted up their eyes, they saw no one but Jesus alone."* (Matthew 17:1-8).

This supernatural event is recorded in Matthew 17:1-8, Mark 9:2-8, and Luke 9:28-36. Peter, John, and James were present to witness the transfiguration. Undoubtedly one reason Jesus wanted them to experience this event was in order to be witnesses to it later. It is difficult to describe in language what happened to Jesus. It was as though Jesus was suddenly and supernaturally changed into His heavenly body. Something almost like the eternal Resurrection took place. Perhaps it was a taste of what His appearance would be after the Resurrection. Perhaps it was a taste of what happens to us in our Resurrection. The fact that Moses, representing the Law, and Elijah, representing the Prophets, were present and conversing with Jesus may be seen as Jesus being the Kingdom fulfillment of the Law and the Prophets.

Remember: Our transformation is meant to be finally a Transfiguration.

106. Transformation: *"I beseech you therefore, brethren, by the mercies of God, that you present your bodies a living sacrifice, holy, acceptable to God, which is your reasonable service. And do not be conformed to this world but be transformed by the renewing of your mind, that you may prove what is that good and acceptable and perfect will of God."* (Romans 12:1-2).

Romans 12:2 calls for people to be "transformed." It is the same word that is used of Jesus as being "transfigured" and is a better translation than transformed. The word "transfigured" interpreted as transformed, is found only in these two places in the New Testament. The underlying belief is that by the power of God a person can undergo a radical change that will result in a new person who has the holiness of heart and life. A new and changed person. 2 Corinthians 3:18 describes believers as changed into the same image of Christ. The change is affected by the power of the Holy Spirit. The Holy Spirit is indispensable in our being transformed into maturity, sanctification, holiness, or righteousness.

Remember: Jesus was transfigured and we are called to be transfigured into His image.

107. Trinity: *"When He had been baptized, Jesus came up immediately from the water; and behold the heavens were opened up to Him, and He saw the Spirit of God descending like a dove and alighting on Him. And suddenly a voice came from heaven, saying, 'This is my beloved Son, in whom I am well pleased.'"* (Matthew 3:16-17). *"And Jesus came and spoke to them, saying, 'All authority has been given to Me in heaven and on earth. Go therefore and make disciples of all nations, baptizing them in the name of the Father and the Son and the Holy Spirit.'"* (Matthew 28:18-19). *"For there are three that bear witness in heaven: the Father, the Word, and the Holy Spirit; and these three are one."* (1 John 5:7).

The word *Trinity* is not itself found in the Scriptures although the word has been found in Christian theology from earliest times. The word *Trinity* expresses the unity of the three in one: Father, Son, and Holy Spirit, the three that come from what is called the Godhead, the One True God. Although the word *Trinity* is not explicitly found in the New Testament, it is there implicitly in regard to the relationship of God the Father, God the Son, and God the Spirit. *"And Jesus came and spoke to them, saying, "Go therefore and make disciples of all the nations, baptizing them in the name of the Father and of the Son and of the Holy Spirit."* (Mathew 28:19–20; 2 Corinthians 13:14; Hebrews 6:1–8). The word itself comes from the combination of two words, *tri-unity,* which means "three united" or "three in one." The classical, historical teaching on the Trinity declares that God is one in substance or being, but that there are three essential and distinct representations of His Person, essentially three persons. It does not mean there are three Gods, but that the one God also reveals Himself through the Son and through the Holy Spirit. Historically, this has been the teaching of all Christendom, except some of the smaller branches or sects of Protestantism.

Remember: There are three separate and distinct persons with whom we are meant to relate, Father, Son, and Spirit.

108. Truth: *"And the Word became flesh and dwelt among us, and we beheld His glory, the glory as of the only begotten Father, full of grace and truth."*(John 1:14). *"Jesus* *said to them, 'I am the way, the truth, and the life. No one comes to the Father except through Me. If you had known Me, you would have known My father also; and from now on you know Him and have seen Him.'"* (John 14:6-7). *" . . .if indeed you have heard Him and have been taught by Him, as the truth is in Jesus; that you put off, concerning your former conduct, the old man which grows corrupt according to deceitful lusts, and be renewed in the spirit in your mind, and that you put on the new man which was created according to God, in true righteousness and holiness."* (Ephesians 4:17-24).

One of the great challenges of life is the desire, need, and importance of trying to discover "what is true and what is false." John 18:37-38 records part of the conversation between Jesus and Pontius Pilate in which Jesus says He has come *"to bear witness to the truth,"* meaning God's truth. Pilate then says, *"What is truth?"* Commentators have long had different opinions about Pilate's question. One interesting interpretation is that Pilate was asking a serious question. What is truth here? In other words, what is real here? It was as though Pilate was trying to understand what was really happening here. This perspective is interesting and has validity since the Orthodox Catholic Church maintains that Pilate and his wife became Christians. What is truth, what is reality, are decisive questions and answers. John describes Jesus as being the fullness of grace and truth (John 1:14-17). Jesus speaks the truth and because of this the Jews seek to kill Him (John 8:40). This was a confrontation between Jesus and the devil who has no truth in him (John 8:44-46). Finally, Jesus describes

Himself as *"the way, the truth, and the life."* (John 14:6). When Jesus is gone He will send the Helper, the Spirit of truth. (John 14:17).

Remember: The truth of reality about us, the Trinity, the world, and where true life is found is found in Jesus and the truth of the Christian faith and life, the written Word of God.

109. Two Natures of Jesus: Jesus was fully human. The Bible affirms that statement that Jesus was both fully human and fully divine, as well as by the Seven Ecumenical Councils and the three Ecumenical Creeds of the One, Holy, Catholic, and Apostolic Church. The Gospels are abundantly clear that Jesus was human. Jesus was born of a woman (Matthew 1:18-25; Luke 2:1-7); Jesus was hungry (Matthew 4:2); Jesus was tired (John 4:6); Jesus experienced sorrow and pain (John 11:35, 38); Jesus struggled with agony (Mark 14:32-4; Luke 12:50; Hebrews 5:7-10). Jesus was tempted (Luke 4:1-13). Jesus also suffered the scourging and the crucifixion (Matthew 27:26-56; Mark 15:15-41). **Jesus was fully divine**. Jesus referred to Himself as the Messiah, the Christ (Mark 8:27-30; 14:61-62). Jesus referred to Himself as the Son of God (Matthew 11:25-27, Mark 12:1-9;1 Corinthian 15:27, Philippians 2:9-11, Colossians 1:16-17). Jesus was declared preexistent (Philippians 2:6, Colossians 1:15-16). Jesus was declared Creator (Colossians 1:16). Jesus had the "very nature" of God (Philippians 2:6). Jesus was the "image" of God (Colossians 1:15, 2 Corinthians 4:4). Jesus was referred to in numerous incidences as "God" (John 1:1, 20:28, Romans 9:5,

2 Thessalonians 1:12, Titus 2:15, Hebrews 1:5-8, 1 John 5:20). *See Jesus.*

Remember: Jesus was fully human and fully God. Meaning, as fully human, He knows and feels what we are experiencing because He was there and being fully God, He has the authority and power to help us become like Him in His holiness and righteousness.

[U] **110. Unpardonable Sin:** (Jesus said) *"Assuredly, I say to you, all sins will be forgiven the sons of men, and whatever blasphemies they may utter; but he who blasphemes against the Holy Spirit never has forgiveness, but is subject to eternal condemnation."* (Mark 3:28-29).

The concept of the "unpardonable sin" is found specifically in Matthew 12:31-32, Mark 3:28-29, and Luke 12:10. It reflects an attitude of the mind and heart that continually rejects and denies the Presence of God in Christ and of His authority. It does not refer to any one particular act. We can always have the opportunity to repent of our sin, whatever that sin may be, and subsequently change our behavior. It is a blatant hostility to Jesus even after one has heard the gospel of Jesus Christ and a person who still hardens the heart so that repentance is not possible.

Remember: With repentance all sins are forgivable. Our continued refusal to obey forces God's judgment.

[V] **111. Virgin Birth:** *"So all this was done that it might be fulfilled which was spoken by the Lord through the prophet saying, 'Behold, the virgin shall be with child, and bear a Son, and they shall call His name Emmanuel, which is* *translated, God is with us.'"* (Matthew 1:22-23). *"Now in the sixth month the angel Gabriel was sent by God to a city of Galilee named Nazareth, to a virgin betrothed to a man whose name was Joseph, of the house of David. The virgin's name was Mary."* (Luke 1:26-27). *See Mary, mother of Jesus and Incarnation.*

[W] **112. Witness**: *"And John bore witness, saying,'I saw the Spirit descending, and He remained upon Him. And I have seen and testified that this is the Son of God.'"* (John 1:32, 34). *"And it is the Spirit who bears witness, because the Spirit is truth."* (1 John 4:6). *"To Him all the prophets witness that, through His name, whoever believes in Him will receive remission of sins."* (Acts 10:43). *"And we are witnesses of all things which He did both in the land of the Jews and in Jerusalem, whom they killed by hanging on a tree. Him God raised up on the third day, and showed Him openly, not to all people but to witnesses chosen before by God, even to us who ate and drank with Him after he rose from the dead. To Him all the prophets witness that through His name, whoever believes in Him will have remission of sins."* (Acts 10:39-43). *"For 'whoever calls on the name of the Lord shall be saved.' How then shall they call on Him in whom they have not believed? And how shall they believe in Him of whom they have not heard? And how shall they hear without a preacher? And how shall they preach unless they are sent?"* (Romans 10:13-15).

To witness is basically the privilege and responsibility of every Christian to give an articulate, comprehensive, self-tested account of the Christian faith that is within us. First Peter 3:15 says: *"... always be ready to give a defense to everyone who asks you a reason for the hope that is in you, with meekness and fear."* How we live our lives—every word, thought, action—is a witness to our faith. Additionally and of prime importance is the fact that we must have the ability to verbalize to any person who needs to find Christ how we meet Jesus and what difference God has made in our lives. A witness proclaims the Good News of the Gospel of Jesus Christ. The idea of witness appears in both the Old and New Testaments. It is used in connection with the taking of an oath (Genesis 21:30). In some cases, God is said to be a witness (1 Samuel 12:5; Romans 1:9). Witnesses are necessary in legal matters (Numbers 35:30; Jeremiah 32:10). In the Fourth Gospel the legal witness idea is used in connection with Jesus' person and claims (John 5:31; 8:13). The same Gospel presents John the Baptist as a witness to Jesus. In fact, witness to Jesus as the Son of God is John the Baptist's sole function in the Fourth Gospel (John). The term is applied to one who testifies to God (Isaiah 43:9–12) and to the work of Christ (Luke 24:48). It is applied, further, to the men of faith listed in Hebrews (Hebrews 11:4–12:1). An important expression of "witness" is the death of the martyr. The martyr witnesses through his death (Revelation 17:6). In Revelation 1:5, Jesus is called "the faithful witness." But the word *martyr* in the Greek is the same as that for "witness." It is easy to see how the idea of martyrdom passes over into the concept of witness. Jesus Himself was the proto-martyr. Stephen, Polycarp, and the long line of the martyrs whose blood became the "seed of the Church" testified to the leadership of Christ, and so became witnesses to the faith. In addition to the witness of the martyrs, and in fact the more normal method, was the witness made through preaching. The word *evangelion* means "good news," and for the Christians the Good News, "the Gospel," was the redemption God had wrought through the event of Jesus: His life, death, and resurrection, in other words the Kingdom of God. The importance of early Christian preaching in this regard is plainly stated by Paul in his letter to the Romans (Romans 10:14). As time passed, the message of the Christian Church needed consolidation. In the second century, the Church was faced with the threat of heretical (wrong or destructive understanding) movements. We see in the Pastoral Epistles (1 and 2 Timothy and Titus) an attempt to state the "true faith" in the face of heretical threats. In the latter part of the second century there was an increasing attempt to state the faith in terms of the apostolic norm. The true faith was thought to be apostolic faith. In that period the witness of the Church was a witness in terms of what was considered to be early and apostolic proclamation. The instinct of second-century Christians in looking to the classical or New Testament period for the normative Gospel was true enough. Departure from it represents a perversion of Christian witness.

Remember: There is no more powerful "witness" than each of us telling our personal story of what God in Christ has done for us.

113. Word of God: *"In the beginning was the Word, and the Word was with God, and the Word was God."* (John 1:1). *"I now rejoice in my sufferings for you, and fill* *up in my flesh what is lacking in the afflictions of Christ, for the sake of His body, which is the church. Of which I became a minister according to the stewardship from God which was given to me for you, to fulfill the word of God."* (Colossians 1:24-25). *"For the word of God is living and powerful, and sharper than any two-edged sword, piercing even to the division of soul and spirit, and of joints and marrow, and is a discerner of the thoughts and intent of the heart. And there is no creature hidden from His sight, but all things are marked and open to the eyes of Him to whom we must give an account."* (Hebrews 4:12-13).

The Hebrews understood the power of words. In essence, they believed that words once spoken took on a life of their own. Everyone can understand the power of a spoken word, whether it be an encouraging word or a degrading word. The impact is powerful and most often lingering. In the Old Testament there is the phrase "the word of the Lord," which is found literally several hundred times and its variance several hundred more. The "word of the Lord" signified a message from God to a person or to God's people, the Israelites. The most common spokespersons or messengers for "the word of the Lord" were the prophets. In the New Testament, the use of "word" is equivalent to the Old Testament understanding in that it signifies a message from God. However, it has expanded to include the Christian message of Jesus Christ. *"On the next Sabbath almost the whole city came together to hear the word of God."* (Acts 13:44). The phrase "the word of God" or its equivalent is found about 400 times in the New Testament. The easiest way to understand the concept is to think of a framework of three expressions of "the Word of God." One is that Jesus is the Word of God. *"In the beginning was the Word, and the Word was with God, and the Word was God."* (John 1:1). In this case, Jesus Himself embodies "the word." The second expression is the "written word" because it contains the Gospel, the doctrine, the teaching of the "words" of Jesus. Jesus said, *"Heaven and earth will pass away, but My words will by no means pass away."* (Matthew 24:35). In 2 Timothy 3:15–16, we read, *"...and that from childhood you have known the Holy Scriptures, which are able to make you wise for salvation through faith which is in Christ Jesus. All Scripture is given by inspiration of God."* The third expression is the "spoken word." *"So it was, as the multitude pressed about Him to hear the word of God."* (Luke 5:1). *"...and they were all filled with the Holy Spirit, and they spoke the word of God with boldness."* (Acts 4:31). *"Now this is the word which by the gospel was preached to you."* (1 Peter 1:25).

Remember: The Living word, Jesus; the written word, the Bible; the spoken word; preaching, teaching, and witnessing.

114. Works: *"Then Jesus said to His disciples, 'For the Son of Man will come in the glory of His Father with His angels, and then He will reward each according to his works.'"* (Matthew 16:27). *"And if you call on the Father, who without partiality judges according to each one's work."* (1 Peter 1:17). *"And behold, I am coming quickly, and My reward is with me, to give to every one according to his work."* (Revelation 22:12).

The "works" concept is one of the most controversial and misunderstood in explaining New Testament theology. However, it is important to grasp what the Bible says about "works." Firstly, it is by faith alone that we are justified before God (Romans 3:26; 4:1-5; Galatians 2:16). Faith is a complete trust of heart, mind, will, and soul to God in Christ Jesus and a total reliance on His promises. It is a complete reliance on God's grace that assures us of our salvation as accomplished on the Cross by Christ Jesus. There is nothing that a person can do to "earn" salvation. Legalism is that arrogant self-righteousness that inwardly believes that "I" have earned my righteousness because of "my" efforts/works. Secondly, all efforts, all "Good works" are those accomplished by the Spirit "working" through us (John 6:29; 1 Thessalonians 1:3; Romans 2:6-7; Acts 26:20). These kinds of works are approved and expected by Jesus (Matthew 16:27; 22:12; 5:16; 7:21; 21:28-43). Works done by us are motivated by gratitude, by love, and by obedience to the Spirit. After all is said and done we can only say, *"We have only done our duty."* (Luke 17:10). Having said all this it must be understood that we will be held accountable for what we have done, in other words our "works".

Remember: Love motivated by gratitude, motivated by faith produces good works that are really not work but a joyful fulfilling of our calling and relationship with the Trinity.

115. Worship: Worship is a very difficult word or concept to easily describe. Literally, the word means to "bow down." Basically then it is an attitude and a behavior that displays love, gratitude, submission, honor, and obedience to the Trinity (John 4:19-24). Jesus says it is not the "mountain" meaning place that is the essential it is that *"God is Spirit, and those who worship Him must worship in spirit and truth."* Acts 2:42 describes how the Christian community worshipped. *"And they continued steadfastly in the apostles' doctrine and fellowship, in the breaking of bread, and in prayers."* And then again James says, *"Pure and undefiled religion before God is this: to visit orphans and widows in their trouble, and to keep oneself unspotted from the world."* (James 1:27).

Remember: Every single thought, word, and action can be a form of worship.

116. Wrath: *"The Father loves the Son, and has given all things into His hand. He who believes in the Son has everlasting life; and he who does not believe in the Son shall not see life, but the wrath of God abides on him."* (John 3:35-36) *"For the wrath of God is revealed from heaven against all ungodliness and unrighteousness of men, who suppress the truth in unrighteousness."* (Romans 1:18). *"But God demonstrates His own love toward us, in that while we were still sinners, Christ died for us. Much more then, having now been justified by His blood, we shall be saved from wrath through Him."* (Romans 5:8-9).

One rarely hears a sermon or teaching on God's wrath these days. It is definitely not a popular subject. We do not want to hear about God's wrath because we do not want to hear about there being judgment or believing there is going to be a judgment day. Basically we do not like the reality of consequences. And yet the Old Testament testifies explicitly to God's anger at sin and disobedience. The New Testament is equally transparent concerning the subject of God's anger at sin, disobedience, and evil. It is the very nature of God's love that wrath is required. It is required of God's people also to *"abhor what is evil."* (Romans 12:9). Some New Testament passages reflecting God's wrath against sin and evil are: Romans 1:8, 2-6, 9:22; Ephesians 5:6; Colossians 3:6; Revelation 6:16; 11:18; 14:10; 16:19; 19:15. *See especially 2 Thessalonians 1:7-9.*

Remember: God's holy love requires compassion and justice. The lack thereof or the presence of sin or evil evokes wrath (righteous anger) and that requires judgment.

RESOURCES

To understand these and other biblical words and concepts with greater depth and clarity we highly recommend *The Standard Sermons of the Reverend John Wesley.*

We highly recommend a concordance of your favorite Bible. Every major Bible translation has an available concordance. (New King James Version, New International Version, New Revised Standard Version, etc.). A concordance is a book that lists all the words of the Bible and biblical passages where that word is used.

Recommended Theological Resources for Additional Study:

- *The Interpreter's Bible, Twelve* Volumes
- Pope, William Burt, *A Compendium of Christian Theology,* Three Volumes
- *The Wesleyan Bible Commentary, Seven* Volumes
- *Clarke's Commentary, Six* Volumes
- *The Works of John Fletcher, Nine* Volumes

Recommended Single-Word Books for Additional Study

- Primary Sources:
- Pope, William Burt: *A Higher Catechism of Theology,* Methodist Episcopal Church

- Vines: *Vine's Expository Dictionary of New Testament Words*
- Vines: *Vine's Concise Dictionary of Bible Words*
- Vines: *An Expository of Old Testament Words*

Secondary Sources:

- Bouyer, Louis: *Dictionary of Theology*
- Manton, M.E.: *A Dictionary of Theological Terms*
- Grenz, Stanley J.: *Pocket Dictionary of Theological Terms*

CPSIA information can be obtained
at www.ICGtesting.com
Printed in the USA
LVHW090309191221
706342LV00001B/36